# Sacred Spiritual Light Leaders

## Worldwide Indigenous Ancestral Healing and Ascension

### A Collaboration

RITZ
BOOKS

Sacred Spiritual Light Leaders:
Worldwide Indigenous Ancestral Healing and Ascension

"MANY PATHS ONE TRUTH"

This book is in honor of the Institute of Whole life Healing, a non-profit organization whose mission is to creatively assist individuals in reconnecting to their Original Greatness, Life's purpose, and Divinity. We seek to offer a path of illumination toward the Source within and offer spiritual sanctuary for those truth seekers who are on the path of enlightenment through service.

We stand on a foundation of African and Native American spirituality in recognition of our shared ANCESTRY and do not desire to isolate, segregate, or confine ourselves to any one ideology...many paths one truth. Lexington, Kentucky is the spiritual home for the Institute and some of the authors of this book, while the book represents mystical stories and themes from around the world.

Our logo is a rainbow-colored labyrinth, representing different sacred paths and entrances that ultimately leads one into self-realization and universal truth. The hands and lotus symbolically lift one into whole life healing and ascension.

Thank you, Priest John Awodele McAtee, for your mandala artwork, as seen recolored throughout this book.

Thank you, Shannon Howard, for designing The Institute of Whole Life Healing's logo, as seen on the cover.

# Foreword
## by Awo Falokun Fatunmbi, Egbe Iwa Pele

This collection of essays gives us a glimpse into the world of spirits, avatars, elevated ancestors, and the frequencies that transmit feelings of inspiration and hope from a wide range of Forces in Nature. This book explains the process through which spiritual light leaders discover their destiny and the need to bring light into the world. They share their journeys of self-discovery as the integration of self-contemplation, guidance from elders and the ability to communicate with ancestors and Spirit of the Earth. It speaks of the way the tools of spiritual light leadership were revealed in the process of a close examination of personal interaction in the workplace.

Through these words, we get a glimpse of how frequency, resonance and vibration can cause an alignment with our higher desires and aspirations. All of these stories of personal growth and inspiration are connected in the ancient earth centered spiritual disciplines rooted in the belief that ancestors, animals, natural elements and mystic visions can be a valuable source of inspiration and wisdom for those who are willing enter the silence to listen and watch for the light of Divine Inspiration. It is a light that has guided humanity from the beginning of recorded history and continues to push consciousness towards deeper levels of understanding self and the world.

To these beacons, we remain grateful.

Good fortune and blessings,
Awo Falokun Fatunmbi, Egbe Iwa Pele

---

You Cannot Be the Light and Hold Another in Darkness
~Paul Selig, The Book of Mastery

---

# Table of Contents

# Meet the Authors

This book is a sacred gift shared with you by some amazingly phenomenal Spiritual Light Leaders. Each chapter will give you just a glimpse of their many paths one truth whole life healing journeys through their writing, poetry, and art, to symphonically assist in your ascension. We are honored to share with you the following authors:

*Queen Mother Osunnike and Priest King Koleoso* – They are the founders of the Institute and the perfect example of divine union. They lovingly encourage all within the community to Know Thyself and look within, question and explore the deepest parts of who we are. They teach us to examine the light and the dark, and how to work on balancing and healing in order to bring our gifts to the world. As loving spiritual parents, they gently guided us along, leading by example, while allowing us to experience our journeys authentically and without intrusion.

*Queen Mother Mariyamah "Olomidara" Sanna* is a phenomenal energy healer and light leader who is committed to ushering humanity into the ocean of love and care with no nonsense affirmations and hugs. She is soulfully devoted to ancient ancestral and indigenous health and wellness practices that we can bathe in at her restorative sanctuary, Harmony and Health in Ghana, West Africa.

*Baba Marshall "Omitosin" Henderson's* unwavering commitment to lead and guide truth seekers who are called to reconnect and evolve their mystic light is engrained within his spiritual and cellular DNA. He is truly a magnetic reflection of his many paths, one truth journey toward ascension.

*Priestess Lisa "AyoDeji" Allen and Ralph L. Stevenson* are the cosmic dynamic duo. AyoDeji offers her gifts to those seeking spiritual transcendence from the hood all the way back to the pyramids. Mr. Stevenson, her father, is a life-long educator and beloved pillar in the Philadelphia community, where his passion to teach shines brightly.

*Priestess Cynthia "Oya Gbemi" Barnes* is a revolutionary transformational light leader who is called to harmonize the sacred and mundane. She is the personification of raw potential and protective innocence as she stands with her feet grounded in the river, while her arms are magnificently swirling true change into existence.

*Priestess Regina "Abegunde" Harris* is a holistically diverse blend of sacred parenting, shamanism, and the martial arts. She is also an advocate for ensuring that our ancient ancestral history is not only remembered; it must be honored and ascended lifetime after lifetime.

*Yeye Gogo Nana (Dr. Aminah Elana Renee Williams Omari)* reflects unwavering ancient ancestral resilience. Nana was truly born with a steadfast commitment to continue uplifting our Enlightened Ancestral wisdom. She is destined to bring forth a new world in honor of the legacy of our ancestors, carrying the torch, while standing on their shoulders.

*Phyllis "Vox Angelus" Douglass* is a Sacred Funnel for the Elohim/Universal Creator and answers her calling no matter what. Vox is the epitome of light beaming forth through her transmissions and the luminous sounds radiating from her voice will lull you into the belly of the Cosmic/Great Mother, for sure.

*Preeti Gupta* is a genuine divinely inspired heart-centered and soulful universal people connector. It is wonderful to observe as she naturally and effortlessly weaves together like-minded mission focused evolutionary do-gooders from different cultures around the world.

*Chief Fuatabong Lekeanju Fonsa Etoke*, not only holds the title and responsibility of a Cameroonian Chief in this lifetime. He is a luminous light leader from many lifetimes who guides one into a harmonic rhythmic dance between the profane and mundane to lift you higher and higher.

# Preface

Our Priest King often shared a quote which ask the question: "Are you going to lead, follow, or get out of the way?" The year 2000 was the formal beginning of our Priest King Babaji Koleoso and my vision to step into our calling as the spiritual leaders for the Institute of Whole Life Healing. Both our Priest King and I have had very diverse spiritual journeys, so, this was an opportunity to integrate the sacred diverse messages from our Many Paths into a unified One Truth. Based on our spiritual journeys we came to know that Indigenous cultures around the world share a "wholistic" view for healing and well-being. We believe that everything and everyone is connected to the whole. Individually, we are like single vibratory notes that connect us to an entire omniversal symphony called Life. The analogy of the symphony, where the collective leads and follows in harmony, which complements each instrument for the whole, is what our mission and philosophy are based on. This realization is what fueled our passion as Priests, healers, and light leaders up to this present day. In all honesty, that journey was not easy. We came to realize that the unified vision of many paths one truth is not for everyone. Our lifelong experience has shown us that this path is for those who have unshakeable faith and innate courage to step outside of our socially and culturally limited conditioned religious boxes. Now, this does not make you special or better; it means that you have a greater responsibility. For she/he who is given much, much is required.

Yes, we in the Institute of Whole Life Healing, will lead the way by example. We will stand as lighthouses in the world shining forth God, Source and Universal light, guiding others to the safety and peace of knowing that this is One Great Web, of which we are all a part of. We will lead the way in the ability to look at the multitude of religious beliefs and extract the unity in all of them. Yes, we will lead the way by example, in our character, in our humility and courage. We will stand on all that the Great Mother is showing us and calling us to, and we will not be moved. The Institute is called to support, guide and lead you along your evolutionary journey into Self-Mastery and ultimately Self-Realization.

We seek to offer a path of illumination toward the Source within and offer spiritual sanctuary for those truth seekers who are on the path of enlightenment through service. We seek to stand on a foundation of African and Native American spirituality in recognition of our shared ancestry and do not desire to isolate, segregate, or confine ourselves to any one particular ideology. We seek to realize the unlimited undifferentiated Source of All Creation, whose Light manifests within each of us regardless of our theological, philosophical, ideological, political, cultural and/or spiritual orientation. We seek to experience union with the Source of All Creation by evolving as fully integrated beings reflecting the One Light of All Creation and honoring and celebrating the unity reflected within all spiritual traditions. We seek to follow the divine truths of our enlightened ancestors while cultivating our own unique gifts from our individual and collectively shared experiences. Realizing that it is all a continuum where the past has formed our present perception of reality, which will create our future. We seek no followers. We seek Divine Union through resurrection, ascension, and illumination.

Our mission is to creatively assist individuals in reconnecting to their Original Greatness, Life's Purpose, and Divinity. Our mission is manifested through a wholistically designed Mind/Body Soul/Spirit (MBS) blueprint based on three key universal principals: *Know thyself. Cleanse and purify. Live in alignment with absolute truth.* These fundamental principles are used to activate the transmutational process for individual and planetary transformation and healing. They are the foundation for the Institute's Ase Whole Life Healing System, Initiations, individual healing sessions, professional training, lectures, retreats, sacred pilgrimages, symposiums and conscious-raising theatrical, and film showcases.

Over the years, we have been blessed and honored to not only share our gifts, practices and calling with thousands of truth seekers around the country and the world. We have also been honored to work in diverse unified collaborative venues, such as this Sacred Spiritual Light Leaders book that you are about to delve into. Now, lets delve into our Priest King's download on Spiritual Leadership...

# Introduction

## This book is in honor of Priest King Nwa Chukwu Nashid "Koleoso" Fakhrid-Deen Karade Eri (1949-2020)

Priest-King, Nwa Chukwu Nashid "Koleoso" Karade Eri; most affectionately called Baba ji Koleoso was the CEO and co-founder of the Institute of Whole Life Healing. Baba ji Koleoso was well known and respected for his willingness to follow his spirit's direction and his soul's timeless wisdom. In his own words, he "seeks to pierce the illusion of matter and become conscious of his divinity." In 2018, he was officially Coronated by Eze A.E. Chukwuemeka-Eri and held the position of Priest King within our Spiritual Kingdom. Baba ji Koleoso was also initiated in the West African Yoruba tradition as a Priest of Shango and High Priest of Orunmila (Babalawo).

Baba ji Koleoso exemplified what he taught; he was Iya Osunnike's divine counterpart, her other half. To watch them dance over the years as cosmic soulmates is truly inspirational. Baba ji, a college administrator, had many powerful and thought-provoking sayings gathered during his journey, and he shared them with us often. Although, Baba ji Koleoso transitioned in 2020, he is still very much alive in the spiritual realms, and he continues to guide us from the other side.

This introduction is one of the many writings that our Priest King downloaded and transcribed over the course of 35 years as a channel for Ra Bena Saa Tur, the Ascended Ancestor of Ancestors. This channeled reading structured in a "master student" format speaks to the questions regarding spiritual leadership that the student is now finding himself in need of answers to. Throughout this conversation it is highlighted that Spiritual Leadership is not an easy achievement. It requires a higher frequency of responsibility, which means the ability to respond from an ever-evolving place.

Humanity is being called to step in and step up from a higher frequency to co-lead in grace and harmony. That calling most importantly is to step into your own sense of knowing who you are at the highest frequency and the highest vibration possible. We are being called to stop letting others define who you are and why you are from a place of competitive power and divisiveness.

The master guides the student in a conversation designed to take one deep inside your wisdom container where you may already know the answers. This master student dialogue becomes an opportunity to rediscover how to be a sacred spiritual beacon of light for others, who may also be struggling in the dark with these leadership questions.

---

The man is the head, but the woman is the neck that turns the head.

Love a woman and she'll make you a king. Respect a woman and she'll make you a God.

A man should be made of velvet and steel.

The women work the magic while the men guard the door.

Remember to be gentle with yourself and enjoy the journey.

~ Baba Koleoso

---

# Spiritual Leadership
## by Priest King Babaji Koleoso

*With the Name of God, Most Gracious, Most Merciful and in the Presence of Our Ancestors, both Seen and Unseen*

"It has been the misfortune of every great teacher that, while he speaks from his level of consciousness, his followers can only receive his message on their level; and the gulf between the teaching and understanding grows wider with time."

~Maharishi Mahesh Yogi

The years have passed, and the student found himself trusted into the position of leadership, but what is a leader and did the student have the qualifications? Many run to the front wanting to be leaders but so few have what it takes to make the commitment for the long haul. The student came to realize that wisdom was needed, and he knew where to go, to his Master.

*Master:* So, you are at the stage of leadership?

*Student:* How did you know?

*Master:* We have watched as you have been placed through some severe trials and yet you continued to get up and move forward, this is an essential quality of a leader – to stay the course.

*Student:* So many seemed to have those qualities, I am one among many?

*Master:* No, you are the one, among many, for few really know God as you know God. They think it is making the will of others submit to you, such is not the case. A leader inspires in others to move forward. Leaders lead, not so much by example but by spirit.

*Student:* Is this why so many of the yogis and gurus seem so unorthodox in this movement?

*Master:* Yes, spiritual leadership is different than secular leadership. A spiritual leader follows spirit and cannot be subdued by the leadership style of others, they must follow God's leadership and that is so different. Dear One, you know where you are going, and you know how to get the people there, so you must have faith that we are with you. Everyone is looking to you and this should not be, they should be looking to God and only God and should be able to see God in you.

As a spiritual leader you must die to being you and are reborn in God consciousness. You have to have the ability to look deep into the lives of others and help them to become liberated souls. Many will become impatient with you and will leave because they are running to what they think is right, but you must understand that God cannot be hurried. God is the author of time, master of time and giver of time, so let them run and go where they choose for all roads lead to God.

*Student:* I ran into this concept of "Dharma' and "Dharma Leader", what does dharma mean?

*Master:* Dharma, means "The essential nature or duty of the living being."

*Student:* My essential nature?

*Master:* Yes, your essential nature is God embodied as you. Thus, the role of a Dharma Leader is that of teacher, we come to teach you of your essential nature but you and only you can experience it.

A dharmic leader in many respects is like a revolutionary, a spiritual revolutionary. A dharmic leader must always be working to bring in a higher consciousness and awareness of who and what we are. As such the Dharmic leader must reach the reality of who and what we are and help others to do the same.

*Student:* Is this like promoting an uprising against the government or establishment?

*Master:* No, it is much more refined. What we speak of now is an internal quest of the individual to find or reach their Self-realized identity and once having done so to help others do the same.

*Student:* I meet so many who claim to know the way and want to teach it, but do they really know it?

*Master:* That is and always will be the case, for many feel it and get excited and are ready to run and teach and liberate the world. Such is good but is dangerous, because we are talking about reaching the ultimate freedom a person can attain and this often requires going down many dark paths.

*Student:* Is this the shadow that so many speak of?

*Master:* Not only is it the shadow, but it is also the path of spiritual death; because you must be ready to accept some of the karma of those you lead and teach. That means a spiritual leader must always be working on his or her spiritual development so that they may stay in touch with the spiritual dimension and lessen the effects of the karma of those they lead. Staying in touch with the spiritual dimension is the leader's foundation and the basis of insights and his/her motivation for helping others. Without a connection to the spiritual dimension a spiritual leader knows he cannot be free enough to lead others to the same freedom.

*Student:* Is this why many spiritual leaders run from it?

*Master:* Yes, for they see the enormity of it, they feel the weight of it and most of all they fear trying to do it without a connection to the spiritual dimension and God.

A spiritual leader must know how to free others from this prison of false aims and ideals, which is such a major part of this materialistic life. The kind of freedom that you as a spiritual leader seeking to lead others to can only be experienced. You must work to help free others from earthly illusions and find ways to deliver the higher purpose of life in ways that people can understand. This must include everyone, so no one is left behind. What is being said now is that all forms of discrimination are excess baggage on this spiritual path.

Thus, you begin to see that you live for the benefit of others. Let us repeat that – you live for the benefit of others. Most come to the path for personal benefit but in time they come to realize that once they move into spiritual leadership that you live for the benefit of others. Dear One, this is such an important and liberating concept, to live for the benefit of others implies selflessness, and to be selfless is to be liberated, i.e., to BE God consciousness!

In one of Rumi's poems it is said, "A lover asks the beloved, how much do you love me? The reply was, I have died to myself and now I live only for you." We as spiritual leaders must die to self so we can live for God through others.

*Student:* So as spiritual leaders we are trying to free others from this limited dimension of existence?

*Master:* Not only are we trying to free them but at the same time elevate them to a higher state of spiritual reality. We need to understand at some point that material existence is like a temporary dream of which we must wake up from so we can be free.

*Student:* How important is understanding spiritual culture?

*Master:* How important is breathing? As spiritual leaders we must fully understand the importance of the spiritual path, spiritual culture and lifestyle and follow it appropriately and show by example how others can benefit from it. Remember, Jesus was walking the water, his example showed Peter what he could do as well, but Peter lost faith! Be the example and do not lose faith.

*Student:* Does this imply some form of education?

*Master:* Proper education in regard to spiritual culture and philosophy is very important. We need to know how to respond to questions in a dignified and enlightened manner. We need to know how to deal with practical issues, and help humanity evolve. We must know how to educate others, so they understand in the manner that is best for them.

This brings to mind again, Jesus saying to his disciples, "Go forth and be ministers to all nations", this is implying that the disciples had to be well versed in the cultural norms of the people they were ministering to.

As spiritual leaders we too must be very well versed in the cultural norms of the people we are ministering to. Our natural tendency is to want to be 'heavy and impressive'. The point I am making here is that if people do not understand the knowledge, they will not remember it and if they do not remember it, they will not apply it in their lives.

It is as the Honorable Elijah Muhammad once said, "we must make it so plain that even a baby can understand it." Thus, the importance of receiving spiritual knowledge from a spiritual leader who has cultivated such knowledge from the proper sources and is also experienced and self-realized knows how to explain it in practical terms. Yes, this is most important. In short, how qualified is your teacher?

*Student:* What of ritual and ceremonies?

*Master:* Spiritual leaders must be able to explain the rituals, customs, and ceremonies to others and not just go through the motions. We must be able to explain purpose, the how's and whys, the reason for and what is going on. We must be able to explain the objective of the ritual and the benefits to be gained for doing it. This must be done in a manner that the people can comprehend its purpose. If such is not followed, then the rituals will not be appreciated and forgotten and given up.

*Student:* Master, what about being inventive along this path?

*Master:* That is a very good question, for this path is ever changing and many are coming to the path with grandiose ideas and wanting to change things. Yet, spiritual leaders must not be afraid to be inventive and seek to try new things for everything is possible. We make this thing too hard; we must try new ways to infuse the message of spiritual cultural teachings in a way that is enjoyable. We must make the teachings enjoyable for young and old alike; we must seek to get beyond making the message boring and dull. God is alive and the message must be alive. Yet, there are guidelines and divine laws that must be respected and followed. The Ancients laid the trail to God realization, all we must do is follow their trail and broaden it for those coming behind us.

*Student:* It seems that the world has fallen under darkness, as a spiritual leader what can we do to dispel the darkness?

*Master:* You must seek to bring spiritual energy and God's love to the battlefield of darkness verses light! You see we must become complete and whole and not be controlled by the darkness of materialism and all of the negative conditions that come with it, such as anger, jealousy, envy, hate, competition and prejudice, and the list goes on.

In fact, these are the properties associated with the Ajogun as found in the Yoruba Ifa faith. We must become a hollow bone so God's love can flow through us. We as spiritual leaders must be ready to fight and fight hard the negating forces of the Ajogun. You see many are not ready to face these traits within themselves. They come to the path full of fire ready to take on the world, little do they realize that the world they must take on is the world of self.

Just because you are a leader does not mean all of your challenges will disappear. Far from it, your challenges will grow as you grow. This is one place where many will fall, because they are looking for fairy tales and happy-ever-after endings without the hard work.

*Student:* Sounds like this path is not for the weak and lazy.

*Master:* Dear One, once you place your foot on this path you must be ready to work and work hard, for God is hiding in you as you and it is hard work discovering this fact. What are you going to do when the Divinities invite you to the 'theater performance' starring you? As you sit in the front role eating your 'ego' flavored popcorn, they show you what a fake you are, they let you know you are not who and what you think you are, they show you clearly the areas that need to be dealt with. What will you do? Yes, they will let you see the beauty of this path, the joy and greatness, but they must show you it is not a game!

People will follow you; they will trust you; they will place their lives in your hands and as a spiritual leader you have to be ready for this. So many come to the path ready to lead the way, ready to initiate others. Little do they know that once you initiate someone, once again, you must suffer some of their karma.

*Student:* Is that the reason the ancients were so cautious in picking devotees?

*Master:* That is one important reason. While many will come with leadership abilities, they may lack the ability to go the long road, this is a lifetime journey, not a one-night stand (smile). Being a spiritual leader requires sacrifice, sacrifice of the first order.

*Student:* Why is that?

*Master:* You must be willing to sacrifice your own selfish desires and longings for the good of the whole and those that follow you. As a spiritual leader you must be beyond suspicion of inappropriate behavior, activities, or association. You must act in a way to be free from rumors or the appearance of improprieties. Temptation will be all around you and you as a leader must realize the 'eyes' are on you. Not so much as looking for faults as it is looking for guidance. Many will be confronted with situations they are not familiar with, and they will be looking to you for assistance. They cannot find you in the same hole that they have fallen in! Those who are blessed to escape must teach and show others the way. We all will be tested to see if we are worthy to enter the inner Kingdom of God–Realization.

As a spiritual leader you must realize while men and women are of the same spirit, they are in different bodies which have different needs. There is a cosmic attraction between male energy and female energy, even in same gender relationships, the energy is still the same, male energy is attracted to female energy. It is this attraction that is constantly seeking to express itself and said attraction must be respected.

Let us end for now on that note. Love yourself as we love you. Ra Bena Saa Tur ancestor of ancestors channeled through our Priest King Babaji Koleoso

## Learn More about
## The Institute of Whole Life Healing
https://www.manypaths1truth.org/

## Donate to The Institute of Whole Life Healing
https://www.paypal.com/donate/?hosted_butt on_id=9EZBSJUX2T5YY

# Cosmic Particles of Sound Frequency Lighting Up the World

## Robin Osunnike Scott-Manna

Our universe is undergoing an evolutionary and planetary shift into higher dimensional frequencies. This ascension is calling humanity to usher in an ancient new unified light.

I'm sharing with you a snippet of my spiritual light journey. Which is about embodying the sacred higher frequencies of unity and harmony, even during the struggles of balancing the light and the dark. When I speak about light and dark, I'm not just talking about race, good, bad or day and night. I'm talking about how I came to reexperience being the universal reflection of the particles, atoms, frequencies, and star systems; believe it or not that we truly are.

During my spiritual journey and reawakening to my Original Divinity, so many wonderful things were being repeatedly revealed. However, I would find myself from time to time – dancing around the inability to honor and live in alignment with my sacred light frequency.

Finally, through the unwavering blessings of the Ancient Mothers I came to realize how the shadow of lies imprinted within our cellular blueprint can keep us replaying the same distorted storylines encapsulated within our "Labyrinth of Self-Circle of Life". Yes, I was able to transmute the ancient fire shut up in my bones, embody my inner luminosity, through sacred resonance and entrainment. Again, this is a snippet to support you in knowing your infinite light I AM frequency and tuning into the essence of you from the inside out.

# I AM

*In the beginning...was the Sound*
*ushered forth from the stillness*
*encased*
*with-in the darkness...*
*Motionless...a feather*
*descending*
*My essence - pure - dark - light*
*lit from within...*

*Illuminated*
*my soul*
*transcends*
*the portals within my mind...*

*Silence echoes*
*a pulsating rhythm*
*vibrating*
*with a resonance so familiar*
*yet unknown...*

Take me higher, lift me higher. I Am light, I Am light, I Am love emanating through the magical mystery of light. Can you hear, taste, feel, smell, and see the light of you? Listen to your light beaming radiance. Whether 528 or 825 hertz hear and feel `the magic of your splendor. Each particle of you is splendid splendor. Radiant, magnificently radiant and every planet, galaxy, and star system, including you has a vibrational frequency.

---

It is necessary, while in darkness, to know that there is light somewhere; to know that in ONESELF, waiting to be found, THERE IS LIGHT.

James Baldwin

---

Wow! Little did I know back then that I, you, we, me, are made of the sound frequencies that give birth to light. It took me a while to really get what the Ancient Mothers, my spiritual guides we're downloading and uploading into my ears on a whole other level about my/our light essence. Really, coming into the knowledge that we are cosmic sound frequencies of light in a human body temple is amazing. From the time I was a little girl, I loved the sound of music from different genres. Delicious sounds and rhythmic motions to this day bring me into higher states of ecstasy. When I was a child, one of the songs I had to sing in our church choir was "This little light of mine, I'm gonna let it shine. This little light of mine, I'm gonna let it shine. This little light of mine, I'm gonna let it shine, let it shine, let it shine, let it shine." That song felt dauntingly familiar. Even as a child I could feel something moving inside of me as I sang that song, like it was turning on "this little light" that felt too big and bright for me. Little did I know back then that so many of our songs were translations of higher universal languages of light for human transformation and ascension.

As a teenager, my mother would often say to me that God had blessed me with a special light and that I needed to reflect that light everywhere I go. But you know what... for me as a lighter skinned black woman growing up in Boston back in the day that light stuff had conflicting messages attached to it. In my mid-twenties and early 30's, I began struggling even more with my light because it made me feel different. You see, I knew I was different but at that time saw and felt my difference in a not so good way. I felt like I was a stranger in my own body. I was also struggling emotionally to swim in the social, political, and racial pool of darkness all around me. To get myself out of that darkness and be me, I would spend countless hours listening to and singing R&B music that lifted me higher and higher as a way of finding some light inside of those dark times. Over time I began to experience some kind of light force energy calling me to come home, like I was in a Star Trek movie or something. I began to see, feel, hear, and sense my own unique difference, which felt like it was connected to someplace other than here, and it felt splendidly unique and strangely scrumptious. Little did I know that I was being called to see my light within all the darkness of me, so that everywhere I went, I could let it shine, let it shine, let it shine. This was taking me somewhere deeper and higher...home.

As I bathed myself more and more in this scrumptious light energy, I began actively working as a scrumptious African American Revolutionary Evolutionary light carrier destined to transform a dark oppressive world system. I was being guided to use my poetry, short stories that I had been writing, healing love songs, and my dramatherapy training to re-form how I needed to transform my own personal and societal pain. I also believed that I needed to bridge my artistic work, informal counseling, and my social activism into a Healing Through the Arts evolutionary means for transforming internalized pain, unresolved trauma, suffering, and imposed injustices from the Inside Out.

While in grad school, studying for my master's degree in counseling, I came across a startling statistic stating that 50% of the women killed in the United States were murdered by their husband or boyfriend. That startling statistic compelled me to write my first screenplay (later adapted for stage) called ...*And I Love You Richard* as my thesis while doing my internship at Renewal House, a transformational shelter for women survivors of domestic abuse.

## Renewal House - Providing Me with the Opportunity to Renew ME

Wow... talk about darkness, this work would have sucked the light out of me if it weren't for a divine miracle. Over the course of four years, my time at Renewal House went from an internship to counselor/advocate and later director. However, let's start with me as the counselor and advisory board member. Our longtime executive director and founder of the shelter was retiring. The advisory board had scheduled our first interview with a woman who had very little director skillsets, and on my day off. But I decided to show up anyway. During the interview, even though her responses were not what we were looking for, to me there was something other worldly about her. Her energy seemed to resonate on a higher level. It was like there was an invisible halo around her that softly sang… "this little light of mine, I'm gonna let it shine, everywhere I go, I'm gonna let it shine, especially in this professional interview." Yup, there was this light just glowing from her as I stared at her silently asking, "Who are you"? No, you probably won't be hired for this job. Yet, there's something about you that I need to know more about, and unknowingly I was going to be ushered into my first mystical steps into sacred sound frequency.

When we finished the interview and said, "We'll get back to you". I said, "let me walk you out" and I did. And just as she was getting ready to go down the stairs and we were saying goodbye to each other, I said "excuse me, excuse me, there's something I have to share with you." And she said, "OK is there a problem?" "No, there's no problem. I have a question that I don't even know how to ask." The more she smiled at what I was saying the more this glow was radiating from her. And so, I said, "I don't know if anyone has ever said this to you before, but you have this amazing glow radiating from you. I've never seen anything like that and I'm curious, is that a certain kind of makeup that you wear?" She laughed even more, and said, "Wow, thank you for sharing." I said, "OK has anyone else said that to you?" Her response was, "actually all the time." I said, "So where is this coming from?" She said, "I started having people ask me that same question several years ago when I started my spiritual practice of chanting." "Chanting, did you say chanting?" She laughed again and said "Yes, chanting." So, I said to her "OK, I don't know much about chanting… is it similar to singing? Because if so, I would love to know more. Can I give you a call." And she said, "Absolutely this is in divine order. I'd love to talk to you more about it."

Little did I know that I was getting ready to step into this whole next divine chapter of my life with a Buddhist chant, which took me to a whole new stage of being. After we spoke, she invited me to a Buddhist gathering where I would learn to chant Namu-myoho renge kyo, which I learned meant "Devotion to the Mystic Law of the Lotus Sutra". This mantra was designed to support those who consciously chanted it to change their karma and overcome all obstacles impeding their success and like the Lotus flower, rise out of the mud and allow the light of the Lotus to cleanse and purify its surroundings. Years later I found out that this was the chant that the luminous music legend Tina Turner chanted off stage, which probably helped her not only survive, but thrive after her marital abuse. This sacred chant began helping me experience the nature of intentional sound and how it can recalibrate every fiber of our beingness. Oh yes, I began experiencing the recalibration of me and then some.

## Light and Dark - Becoming ALL of Me

Over the next few years as the director of Renewal House and, continuing to creatively support women survivors of domestic and sexual abuse, I began struggling again with what felt like these contradictions of the lightness and darkness. The light and dark of the world were now going to war as fibroid tumors were taking up residence inside my womb. What on earth am I missing universe?

## Facing My Shadow within My Own Darkness

I was beginning to experience spontaneous other lifetime regressions. These lifetimes seemed to have something to do with short circuiting my light. Then one night during an energy sound healing session that I was resistant to having, I came to realize that I was grieving an ancient sadness that was percolating inside my womb. Grieving the empty spaces between my womb and heart... Grieving not having my divine masculine twin flame... Grieving the dissolving of my sacred feminine power... Grieving those other lifetimes of unexpressed volcanic rage for the violations, desecrations and vicious torturing of my womb and the wombs of my African, Cherokee, African American and European "Ancient Ancestral Mothers".

This raw dissonance was greatly disturbing, and each time consciously or unconsciously revisited, it seemed to plunge me back into the depths of my fragmented perfectly imperfect light.

No matter what, I was determined to continue delving deeper so that I could rise higher into the true essence of me. I began to explore more consciously my own other womb lifetime stories which were within my embodied "Labyrinth of Self" chart that I designed. As I delved deeper, I came to realize that from within the womb of the "Cosmic Mother" and our birth mother's womb we have complete conscious awareness of our "whole self" and all the aspects related to our wholeness. This awareness remains after birth – for a while – that is until we begin the journey of separation into our individual selves.

The process of healthy separation is a part of the human experience but when we lose sight of our wholeness and begin to identify with only the distorted parts of us, we enter a life path that becomes fragmented. The vital aspects of us become lost, hidden, disconnected, repressed, disowned and unacceptable. This becomes the shadow that our light is hidden behind. In addition, each of these electromagnetic yin/yang parts of the self, have many layers – from the most subtle to the densest.

For many, the awareness of this fragmentation and the need to consciously collect these fragmented pieces of ourselves ushers one into the evolutionary process of individuation. This knowledge is the inspiration to begin the journey along the Labyrinth of Self back home to wholeness – the totality of our beingness – and that circle begins within our womb. Our womb, which contains our sacred soul blueprint, not only holds our soul's incarnation agreements, it's also where we can begin to clear away our many lifetimes of accumulated mental and emotional toxic imprints. Once again, the accumulation of this toxicity creates an energetic film that grows into the "Shadow" self – keeping us fragmented and disconnected from our true inner light self and inner knowing. From the Womb of Darkness – ALL Light comes forth. So, I began increasing my sound bandwidth because sound gives birth to light, and the language of music medicine ignites the mind, body, and spirit's natural ability to heal.

Sure enough, I began hearing faint whispers echoing from somewhere deep within me and around me. Soon the whispering voices became piercingly thunderous like silent screams within me.

"STOP! Please," I begged. "Stop screaming! Please! I can't hear you when you scream!" The raspy bodacious roar of this voice was deafening. It bellowed throughout my inner sanctum like a whispered echo riding on a frequency familiar – yet way too far away to comprehend. This was a primordial tone: rich, pulsating, sound vibrating. Older than old, it was ancient. It was what would become, for me, a whole different knowing of God/Source, and it was "Feminine". This was an ancient new knowing for me. And, in the early stages of hearing these voices, I was somewhat scared. And yes, scared or not, I needed to know more about who I Am and these sounds coming through me. I was ready to "experience the truth" about my divine essence – to remember who I really am. And be careful what you ask for because within a flash of light my body began to tremble, and I heard, felt, and fully experienced the echoed whispers of whom I later remembered were "The Ancient Mothers" speaking through me, to me, and to those I was called to help with their healing and transformation.

Breathing deeply and fully, I began to surrender to that now familiar sound and slipped into that ancient abyss that resides between now and infinity – light and dark – feminine and masculine. I was catapulted home, finally – yes home. I started to ascend and remember...

*Within the blink of a thousand eyes, my soul just started to remember. Remember a time beyond before. A time that feels like time and space ceased to exist - a time so indescribable. How do I describe something so incredibly indescribable? A memory of something that is so deeply subtle, expansively profound, massively multidimensional, and yet, so intricately personal that it starkly penetrates the multi-layers of my existence.*

*Memories of something so enchantingly soothing enveloping my heart and rocking my spirit into an ancient abyss of blissful knowing. A knowing that I am encased within my own stellar being experiencing the cosmos stretching before and beyond me in perfect harmony. I remember experiencing atoms exploding into a quiet symphony of sound.*

*And I knew the I AM and that I Am One with the All. Darkness and Light. That was the first time I consciously remembered knowing the frequency of Who I Am...Internal and External Luminosity.*

Over the years, I began tuning into amazing sound healing instruments like tuning forks, crystal and Tibetan bowls, rain sticks and bells. There was just something about them that really resonated and supported the energy healing work with my clients.

One of the things that I really loved doing in my healing sessions was using these sacred instruments along with breath work and high frequency music that helped to draw them into deeper aspects of themselves. I would also use my voice to sound over different parts of their body and pay attention to how those sounds made their body respond. I noticed how their body would either jerk, twitch, or express deep sighs of relief. Often met with deeper breathing, tears that would silently be flowing down their face and/or screams that would come out of the rawness of their bodies. It was amazing! Often, when I would start a session with the client and keep my eyes closed, I could see light beams in different parts of their bodies radiating where there were blockages, and my hands would know exactly where to go. And the sounds coming through me from this dark void would vibrate throughout their entire body. This light work also began assisting me in manifesting my heart-centered wishes and desires. First, to move to Jamaica in the West Indies when I felt a strong calling to provide my healing work at this phenomenal spa right on the beach. Yeah, I had waited forever and a day for this opportunity.

## Jamaica Was All About the Light and...

Being on this beautiful island listening daily to the ocean waves took my sound medicine work to a new level. I put aside my instruments and became aware of the natural elemental sounds of the wind, birds, insects, and the sacred Caribbean Indigenous drumbeats, which along with my voice had an even greater impact on me, and my clients. Whether daytime or nighttime, the mystery and magic wrapped me again in a strangely familiar stroll along the labyrinth of me.

I remember one dark night without any moonlight, I laid out on the ground breathing into the vibration of the earth and once again longing to go home. Where is home? What is home? I thought I was home. Where is this aching in my belly and longing in my heart coming from? And as I laid there, I looked up into the black sky sprinkled with stars, twinkling like some kind of sign language, speaking into my invisible ear. I stared into this luminous darkness and began to see something gliding in the sky like a spacecraft moving in a circular motion. There was a part of me that was mesmerized and another part of me that wanted to take back what I had just said about going home. I mean was this a spaceship coming for me to take me home? I hope not, I think not, but I didn't really know. And am I really seeing what I think I'm seeing?

So, what I decided was just in case let me ask, are you a spaceship? As I spoke this up into the sky, it stopped, and then continued its circular motion as if we were in communication. Then I asked, "if you are really a spaceship, please be still," and it stopped moving. I made the request two more times so I would know whether it was for real or not. The next thing I knew was a cluster of stars near the spaceship began penetrating splendid beams of light into my womb. And I began speaking the light language that had been coming through me for the past few years. The next thing I experienced was being connected to that cluster of stars. And I heard the whispering roar ask the question that still vibrates in and out of me to this day. "Do you know who you are?"

## The Dark… Facing My Shadows Again - Dang

My goodness, what on heaven and earth was Jamaica really about for me? The next morning at the crack of dawn, while doing some yoga postures, I had another major other lifetime remembering. There was a part of me that was remembering what I really didn't want to remember. As I looked out into the ocean, I began going into a spontaneous regression and saw a very old ship coming toward the reef and it was filled with many enslaved ancestors. What on earth was I seeing? Why was I seeing this ship coming into Jamaica with all these enslaved women and men from... Ghana? How did I know this? As I continued journeying back in time, yes, I saw, felt, and knew that I was one of them. I saw myself in shackles and the more I experienced me then, I could feel the throbbing pain between my thighs from the horrific rapes that I had experienced on that ship during that arduous journey.

Through that pain, I began hearing my sobbing turn into a scream of bewildering rage, "How could anyone do this to a woman?" How did this happen to me – a woman who had been a Queen Mother in another lifetime in Ghana that felt like it had been eons ago and yesterday. I was now remembering my journey, my first journey into Jamaica as that enslaved Queen the empowered revolutionary evolutionary Maroon women. As I began to study more about the Jamaican Maroons, I learned that they had been the enslaved Africans who said, "NO, this will not be my destiny." They strategically escaped from the enslavers and journeyed up into the tumultuous regions within Jamaica to acquire and preserve their freedom and sustainability for themselves and generations to come. Again, what was the universe conveying to me? I was a bit of a wreck, so I reached out to a close friend and spiritual intuitive colleague back in the states who could commune with higher star beings to give me some necessary guidance. The following is what they shared with him to share with me.

*Why is Robin in Jamaica? She is in Jamaica to learn how to survive during the earth changes that will prepare her to accept her role as a teacher and healer. She is there to open her doorway to her essence, do not despair, all is at hand, she will do well to accept what is to be learned from this experience. She will need to study the people and learn to deal with the fears of the darkness, unknown into the light, known. She is the dark side, manifesting light which is unknown to others yet is the expression of knowledge, wisdom, and understanding of truths, new truth to be made manifest, yet indisputable. She needs to dwell in the darkness, the fear of the unknown so she can bring out the light. She needs not to despair, but to be at peace, learn from the ways of the populace, and heal their fears.*

*Define the opening of the doorway to her essence: This allows the interaction of her spirit with her physical body. The becoming in the one, she is next to become in the one. She is a role model for humankind, the prototype of human Ascension, in spirit, and in physical form. This is the essence we speak of.*

*The plantation and feelings coming up for her are connected to knowing but not remembering that there was once a colony of slaves in this area. She needs to look to the ocean, look to the caves, look, and she will see, see and she will know, and she will understand, understand, and be one with the land, be the inheritor of the souls, release the fears, and release the souls.*

*Define the elevation of the souls: She is to release the lost souls of her ancestors by finding them, ushering them through the portal of darkness into the light. Allow them to be released by instructing them how to ascend into the light. Use the dark and the light to make the transition of the souls. She must attract the souls into her feminine darkness and direct them toward the masculine light. Release the souls from the darkness of the lack of light, release them to be free from the land of Jamaica, the light and the dark, back into the oneness the all, the star seeds of the universal oneness of all that is.*

## From the Womb of Darkness All Light Comes Forth

Back in the US and fibroids removed, I was blessed with a plethora of miraculously guided opportunities to re-create and rebirth all of me. As a major part of this integration process, I was blessed to miraculously reconnect with my cosmic twin flame, Baba Koleoso in the physical realm. Who knew that this divine masculine light leader would become my sunrise for the next 20 years? Baba was definitely a part of the Perfect Sacred Union cosmic particles I needed in weaving together the Tapestry of My Soul. And through this sacred union harmonizing frequency we co-created and birthed the Institute of Whole Life Healing.

## Ascension and Rebirth...
## Yes, I know who I AM Let it Shine, Let it Shine, Let it Shine

Yes, what else was this sacred copulation of darkness and the light going to produce? As they say today within the "new age" community, there are some things we just can't make up. Here I was in Belgium participating in a weekend Tantric Sacred Sexual Retreat. This profound experience, which I could not make up happened on the last day of the retreat during a sound and breath ceremony. As you have read so far, I thought I knew a lot about the power of sound frequency and breathwork. As I breathed in these higher frequencies of sound being chanted throughout the room, a mystical full embrace of surrender began happening. I felt my body being stretched and pulled like a rubber band through the eye of a needle, tightness everywhere, my body compressing like I had no bones, no vertebra, no spine, just liquid being squeezed through the portal of the Cosmic Mother's womb. Gripped with fear of not being able to breathe, there was a foreign and familiar death that was causing me to surrender deeper, surrender my very breath and this physical life until I was only breathing through her to her with her.

Every contraction was releasing more and more of the human me into total luminous darkness and glistening luminescent beings of light sprinkled throughout a web of this darkness – like the Star Beings. As my heart opened and poured out authentic unconditional love and forgiveness, the shackles from every lifetime were fading out of existence. And with my inner sight, I saw the Cosmic Mother's womb, home, yes home. I was home and the higher sound frequencies echoed and reverberated throughout my entire being as ONE. Within me was a sense of knowing that there was a reconfiguration and integration going on within my head, heart, and womb. A vibratory frequency returning and transfiguring me like the Lotus, as the light poured in from the Cosmic womb of universal darkness. I was realigning with my divine soul frequency blueprint which is my revolutionary evolutionary roadmap for the success of this lifetime journey to contribute to Rebirthing a New World.

# One Million Wombs United – My Light Leader Mission

Our universe is undergoing an evolutionary and planetary shift. This is a time of major healing. Evolution and the momentum is vibrating across the world for us to usher in an ancient new beginning. As we heal and evolve ourselves, we naturally contribute to the healing of the Womb of our Earth Mother and Her family; for one mother's womb is another mother's womb.

---

In Healing Sounds, Jonathan Goldman states:
"Through the principle of resonance, sound can be used to change disharmonious frequencies of the body back to their normal, healthful vibrations."

---

# Sacred Feminine Mysteries
# Spiritual Womb Forgiveness Decree

Oh, Great Mother, holy mother, holy mother. Please hear the whispered echoes of my call. I invoke the essence of your spirit and ask that you assist me in the forgiveness, releasing and healing of all who have trespassed against thy womb, my womb and my ancestral mothers' wombs within this lifetime and all other lifetimes pertaining to this time. So that I may reclaim my feminine power, restore my ancient covenant with the Great Mother, the divine cosmic forces of nature, and rejoin in the resurrection and ascension of all humanity into the Oneness of All Creation.

Great Mother, I am now willing to forgive all who have dishonored my womb.

Great Mother, I am now willing to forgive all who have sexually abused my womb.

Great Mother, I am now willing to forgive all who have raped my womb.

Great Mother, I am now willing to forgive all who have taken from my womb and our Earth mother's womb without return.

Great Mother, I am now willing to allow your golden light of unconditional love and forgiveness to abundantly flow with grace and ease within my heart.

For it is you, oh, my Great Mother who holds up the mirror for me of unconditional love and forgiveness held in perfect balance within your universal heart.

Oh, Great Mother it is my intention to unconditionally love, honor, treasure and adore the sacredness of your universal womb, my womb, my earth mother's womb, my birth mother's womb, and the wombs of my ancestors going seven generations back and I honor the sacred feminine mysteries that have been entrusted into my care for the upliftment of humanity. I Live in Alignment with the Absolute Truth Great Mother of who I AM, the spiritual essence of Divine Love, which has so radiantly and magnificently manifested within me as woman. Yes, I know Great Mother... who I AM

---

"We Cannot Be the LIGHT and Hold Another in Darkness"
Paul Selig

---

## Please Remember

You are able to reconnect to your sacred feminine womb power through sacred sound, breath, movement, and touch. As you breathe, listen, and feel from the inside out, what are you being called to *rebirth*, to bring forth for *you* and *humanity* from the *inside out*? Remembering without apology that birthed from the mystical and magical womb of darkness *you* are a Sacred Feminine powerfully gifted vessel of luminous light here to share your special treasures and uplift humanity... Let's reconnect!

# Queen Mother Osunnike

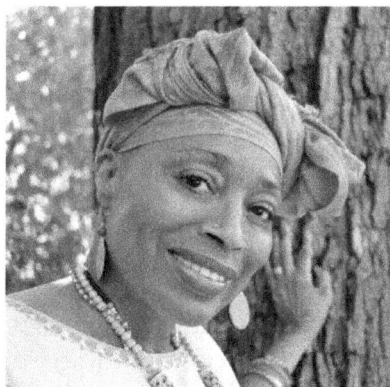

Queen Mother Osunnike Anke is a natural healer, spiritual intuitive/seeress, priestess of the ancient West African Goddess Osun, co-founder, and president of the Institute of Whole Life Healing, a non-profit organization designed to assist individuals and groups in remembering their Original Greatness, Life's Purpose, and Divinity.

She is also the founder of *One Million Wombs United*, and the chief priestess of the Sacred Feminine Mysteries Initiation – Passage into the Great Mother. As a spiritual midwife her mission is to re-ignite the luminous light within the wombs of women across the world. Those women consciously created, chosen, and called to re-awaken the ancient wisdom that lays dormant within their sacred wombs to rebirth a "new world." In addition, her commitment is to support those awakening men to rise up like the lotus no matter what.

Within her heart and soul, she knows that the healing of Mother Earth and humanity rest within the healing and re-integration of the Sacred Feminine and Divine Masculine beginning from the Inside Out.

https://www.osunnikeanke.com
https://www.onemillionwombsunited.org

# The HOOD (Hidden Orishas, Oracles, and Deities) Illuminated

## Lisa AyoDeji Allen

I am the oldest of five children on my mother's side. My brother Shawn, younger by two years, was the third oldest. He was a Philly street soldier, a warrior, a sage, and fiercely protective. I loved him for that. In fact, I admired him greatly. He was one of my greatest teachers and a beautiful soul. Prior to his passing in 2016, in the midst of all he was going through, including drug addiction, homelessness, cancer, and prison, he would always carve out time to write or call and say, "I love you!"

In July 2022, I was videotaping the orbs of light in my home. (Check out my story in the Seed Series book Seed of Destiny published by Steph Ritz for more information about the orbs). As I would do normally, I enlarged the screenshots to see if a face was visible. Sometimes, I would see a face with most being unknown to me. To my delight, this time, I captured Shawn's face six years after his passing.

I teared up remembering how much I miss and love him, while thinking about all the hardships he endured when he was here. My words to him were, I will light a candle for you. His reply, "No need. I am the light." Whoa! I was reminded in that moment a person's circumstances or what they have done, do not define who they are on a soul level. This story is about finding light in the hood and forgiveness.

## The Streets of Philadelphia

I grew up in the hood on the streets of Philadelphia. For those unfamiliar, the hood is typically inhabited by folks of a lower socioeconomic status. In spite of that, or maybe because of it, the sense of community is strong. Back then, in the 60s and 70s, it was much safer than it is now. We were allowed to explore as long as we were home when the streetlights came on. Today, the hood is a much more dangerous place due to the drug abuse epidemic, increased crime, and homelessness, but there are hidden gems, as I expect there always have been, if we are open to receiving them.

I left Philadelphia in 1991. I made my way to Atlanta, Georgia, in search of something new, something different. During my years there, I found spirit or should I say, spirit found me. I also gave birth to an amazing daughter who blessed me with a phenomenal grandson. I married a wonderful man who helped teach me about myself and others. I helped raise two beautiful twin stepdaughters who blessed me with two precious granddaughters and another amazing grandson. I went through three spiritual initiations. I had a multitude of otherworldly experiences and discovered my cosmic connection to the Sirian star system. In Atlanta, I found myself!

After 31 years there, I decided to return to the same house I grew up in. Unbeknownst to me at the time, when I made the decision to return to Philadelphia, I came back to illuminate spirit in the hood and to be illuminated by it.

Returning to live in the family home required a huge shift adjustment for me, as did living in Philadelphia, altogether. Having been away for so long, I had become accustomed to a different vibration and expectation. Philly shook all of that up from day one.

It's bitter cold in late December in Philly and my first day back was no exception. After a 14-hour drive and unloading a 24-foot truck into my storage unit, I made my way to Home Depot to drop off the moving truck. My mind was blown over the way in which many Philly folks navigated their lives on the daily. They were rude, inconsiderate, aggressive, and disrespectful to say the least! It took me a good month or so to recalibrate my frequency. This was an important and necessary step, if I were to successfully navigate and flow here. Once I was able to accomplish that successfully, I began to experience Philadelphia in a different way. I started looking past the exterior, the battle-beaten armor they were wearing in defense of anything and everything that came across their paths. For many Philly folks, this armor is a part of their everyday attire and created from their circumstances and experiences. Once I shifted my perspective, I could see beyond what was hidden behind it. At that moment, I realized Philly was going to be a fantastic teacher.

I was welcomed with open arms by family and friends in the neighborhood. I found this strong sense of community. There seemed to be an unspoken understanding in the hood, "We look out for ours." And, I was one of theirs, even after having been away for so long.

As I walk the Philly streets, I am watched to ensure I am safe and protected in the neighborhood where I was raised. There is honor and respect behind the toothless smiles, tired eyes, and haggard bodies of those who seek a hug after so many years. As I reflect, despite all the darkness I have endured, they see my light, and for that I am grateful. Sadly, they do not see their own, amidst the poverty, crime, broken dreams, and sense of hopelessness. They've been on these same streets for more than 50 years and have resolved themselves to it.

I see them as more than their circumstances. I see them as the gods and goddesses they are deep within. I have my brother Shawn to thank for teaching me to see them with my universal heart instead of my earthly eyes. In spite of the life he lived, Shawn knew who he was spiritually. He would share his wisdom on illumination and ascension with anyone who had the spiritual ears to listen. He taught his comrades in hood all about the Divine Self and our connection to the one source. He understood the light in the darkness. He could recite excerpts from ancient texts effortlessly. He represented the orisha Obatala who is the father of all orisha. Obatala is the white cloth, purity and light. He rules the Ori, which is the head, and one's spiritual destiny.

Shawn, due to his circumstances, had one foot in the dark and the other in the light. He walked between both worlds. Homeless and terminally ill, he purposely committed a crime, so he could be arrested and not die on the streets. In his divine power, he chose when he wanted to make his transition into the other realms. He refused to die in the darkness inside a prison cell. Holding strong, despite the stage four stomach cancer that had spread and prevented him from eating, once he arrived at the hospice facility and was bathed, tended to and dressed in white pajamas, he died shortly after, within hours of arriving. He left this physical plane on his own terms. That's powerful and speaks to who he was as this divine light, a sage in his own right!

## Back Where It All Began

Here I am back in the family house where I grew up with Shawn. I am in the same bedroom I slept in as a child and shared with my sister who is younger by one year. It was here, 38 years ago, I experienced a violent and life-changing loss perpetrated by one lost in the dark. His actions cost him 45 to 90 years in prison and I did not allow his darkness to take my light.

The room seems so much smaller now. It almost feels cave-like which is the perfect setting for going off the grid, metaphorically speaking, to get still and quiet to contemplate my journey thus far.

Walking helps bring me clarity, so I walk often. During a walk to the corner store in the hood, I saw a vulture on the sidewalk. I couldn't believe it. Among the abandoned homes, drug dealers selling their wares on the corner, and trash ridden streets, she was walking along, as if she belonged there, just like a city pigeon. Being older and a bit wiser now, I knew this sighting had a special message for me.

Vultures, typically, get a bad rap but in truth they are powerful messengers. In my journey I have come to learn that vultures represent death and rebirth. Now, how is that tied to the hood? In the most simplistic view, death permeates the Philly air. Death is a way of life here. Philly folks are killing Philly folks every day! Fathers and sons and brothers are dying daily. I cannot count the number of senseless deaths of those I personally know either through family or friends in the hood and it's inter-generational. Spiritually speaking, death of the old and a rebirth into the new is needed in the hood to bring about much needed cleansing, healing and restored balance.

This was a powerful message and a reminder to me to stay the course because I was on the right track. As a student at the Institute of Whole Life Healing, Iya Osunnike and Baba ji Koleoso teach 3 main principles to live by, and they are used to activate the transmutational process.

- Know Thyself
- Cleanse and Purify
- Live In Alignment with Absolute Truth

The vulture reminded me of all three and that I had some more work to do inside and out. Who would have thought a random sighting of a vulture could illuminate so much?

Months after the vulture experience, I was awakened just before dawn. I felt this pull to get up and look out of my bedroom window, which faces the back of the house and an alley. It was still dark outside, and to my surprise, I saw something sleeping right under my window and on the roof of my brother's car. As I squinted my eyes to make out what it was, I was shocked to see a sleeping fox! There was a fox in the hood! My! My! My! What was spirit telling me this time?

The fox represents the ability to see and hear beyond what is physically visible. As an empath, I carry this gift and I was being asked by Spirit to really tune-in and gather the diamonds, the wisdom, being given to me by the hood. As the saying goes, that was "all up in my face" and spirit was getting my attention in very unexpected ways. I'm listening!

Did you know groundhogs hang out in the hood too? I had no idea until one casually walked out of the abandoned lot behind the house. According to Sandra Kynes in her book Llewellyn's Complete Book of Correspondences:

Seeing a groundhog represents astral realms, beginnings, community, consciousness (deep exploration), cycles, death (without dying), dreamwork, family, protection, rebirth/renewal, shamanic work (trance), sleep.

This message resonated with me as I was continuing my work in Philly with the cosmic energies, the lion people called Paschats, from the Sirian star system, who had made themselves known to me two years prior. Understanding our cosmic origins helps to assist us in knowing our true essence as light beings. Did you know we are made up of the same stuff that stars are made from? In addition, this message echoed the death/rebirth message from the vulture, and it speaks to community. Even though the Philly hood is vibrating at a lower frequency, at its core, Philly is all about community. The shamanic work spoke to my work as a priestess and the ability to heal on an energetic level. Hmmm, this thing was getting deeper! I needed to connect the dots.

## Who Am I?

*I am SHE*
*Known by many names*
*The fire that burns in my soul can transmute the World*
*Watch me dance*
*See me step in resonance with the song of the Universe*
*I came here to learn*
*I came here to teach*
*Do you see me?*

*Look past my plain clothes*
*Don't let my un-made-up face fool you*
*For I am a Goddess*
*Queen of the Stars*
*Do you see me?*

*I have gifts to offer the World*
*I am filled with mystery and magic*
*My cup runneth over!*
*Do you see me?*

As a spiritual light leader, I help my clients find their own light using my God-given gifts as an oracle reader, empath and channeler. My gifts allow me the ability to step into one's energetic vibration to determine what energies are present and how to best navigate through perceived obstacles.

One of my favorite stories to share centers around a client who was referred to me. I never met this woman in person, but our connection was powerful. She contacted me via phone for a reading to help provide some, much needed, clarity in her life. She lived in California, and I lived in Georgia. We agreed upon a day and time when she could have quiet and alone time to be still and go within. At that same time, I gathered my spiritual tools to tap in and ask for guidance from her A-team, her guides, guardians, angels, enlightened ancestors, etc.

To my surprise, during the tuning in, I found myself balled-up in the middle of my living room floor in a fetal position and rocking gently with my eyes closed. When my eyes opened, I felt as if I were seeing everything for the first time. I sat up and began to write. Words were flowing through the pen in my hand. This phenomenon is called automatic writing. When the writing stopped, I read it and was blown away.

I contacted my client in California the next day to share my experience, and what was written. I first told her about me being in a fetal position and rocking on the floor. She literally gasped and said, "Oh my God! My mother, before she died, would just lie in the bed and rock in a fetal position." Whoa! I wasn't expecting that. I then asked her if she had any relatives or loved ones who passed away and were blind when they were living. She was sure there were no blind relatives in the family and said she would check with her older sister to be sure.

Lastly, I read to her what had come through during the automatic writing. The key message there was this, "Remember to see with your heart and not with your eyes because what you see with your eyes is an illusion." We spoke a good while about all that had come through. She thanked me and our call ended.

Two weeks later I received a thank you card from her and to my astonishment, she informed me that she discovered, through her older sister, her biological maternal grandmother was actually blind. It turns out the woman whom she thought was her biological grandmother, and who helped raise her, was actually the woman who adopted her mother when she was a baby. What? For more than 35 years, my client never knew this part of her story. Deeper still was the message that her biological blind grandmother brought to her from the other side, "Remember to see with your heart and not with your eyes because what you see with your eyes is an illusion." Her biological grandmother was letting her know, regrettably, after giving birth, she did not see her own child/the client's mother, with her heart. She only saw her baby with her earthly eyes and, as a result, she gave her daughter up for adoption, a decision she obviously regretted. So, deep!

That experience will stay with me forever. It speaks to the power of spirit and the truth that we do not die. We simply transition to another realm. Being able to retrieve that important piece of her own puzzle helped set in motion illumination for that client. How wonderful is that?!

We have to begin seeing ourselves and others not with our earthly eyes but with our universal hearts. I certainly learned so much of this through my brother Shawn's life and transition. Illumination is necessary for growth and evolution. My curiosity piqued; I began to research Philly's roots in an attempt to illuminate the dark truth about the inter-generational trauma that seemed to be a big part of the Philly vibration. What was the source of this trauma?

# Philly's Dark Past

According to Wikipedia:

Enslaved Africans arrived in the area that became Philadelphia as early as 1639, brought by European settlers. When the slave trade increased due to a shortage of European workers during the 1750s and 1760s, approximately one to five hundred Africans were sent to Philadelphia each year. In 1765, there were roughly fifteen hundred Black Philadelphians; of these, one hundred were free. By the time the American Revolution broke out in 1775, enslaved individuals were one-twelfth of the roughly sixteen thousand people who lived in Philadelphia.

We can only imagine the atrocities they suffered at the hands of their enslavers. Now, as I walk the streets of Philadelphia that bare the original cobblestones, where slaves were sold and horse-drawn carriages were the mode of transportation, I try to imagine walking in their footsteps. I began to wonder if any spiritual work has been done to cleanse and lift those lower vibrational energies associated with slavery and left behind from the past. Little did I know, Spirit had something in store for me.

## The Orisha in the Hood

Now, this was the absolute kicker! One day, as I exited the neighborhood grocery store, I walked by a car with a license plate that read Ogbe Osa. Let me point out this license plate is the only one in the entire state of Pennsylvania. Pennsylvania covers 46,055 square miles. Let me also say Ogbe Osa is one of the 256 sacred Odus in the African religion of Ifa. The Odus were written more than 2,500 years ago and are the blueprint of life used to guide humanity towards their destiny. Take that in for moment.

*Ogbe as an expression of spiritual growth represents perfect alignment with destiny. The African deity Obatala speaks through Ogbe. Obatala is said to have descended from heaven on a chain to mold the first humans and indeed to mold every child in the womb.*

*Osa is the manifestation of sudden unexpected change. The African deity Oya speaks through Osa. Oya is the owner of winds and storms, and she brings change, wanted or not, into the lives of humans. She's the fiercest of the female Orishas.*

Obatala is the Divine Masculine and Oya is the Sacred Feminine. This odu shows us the power of Divine Union and was letting me know that coming back to Philadelphia is connected to my spiritual growth as a priestess and change, for both me and Philly, was brewing. Interestingly, since my brother Shawn represented the Obatala energies, I wondered to myself, if he was bringing this odu to me from the other side. Come on! Seeing a sacred odu on the only license plate in the entire state is beyond a coincidence.

As I continued to open myself to the messages being given to me in the Philly hood, I began to realize I was being guided towards something bigger than myself, but what it was, I had no idea. I began to pay attention to my dreams. They were becoming much more lucid. I also found myself revisiting the otherworldly experiences I had over the past five decades. The answer to the real reason for my return to Philly and next steps were in there, somewhere, but where? The answer would require a trip back down memory lane.

## The Institute

In 2011, I found myself at the door of the Institute of Whole Life Healing following my search to find someone who could teach me about two very important things at that time in my journey, with the first being the Iyaami and, the second, divine union of the God and Goddess within.

According to Ifa Global,

In the Yoruba West African language, Iya means 'Mother,' while Ìyámi translates to 'my mother.' The Mothers embody the role as the force of creation, sustainer of life and existence, elevating her to the realm of the infinite divine. The word Ìyámi - in tones becomes Ìyààmi or Ìyàmi, which can translate as the super-powerful ones or my mysterious mother.

Why was I seeking information about the Iyaami? Some 15 years prior, during a trip to New Orleans and a UFO sighting, which you can read about in the Seed Series book, The Seed of Destiny, published by Steph Ritz, I began speaking an African language unknown to me. The same word was always spoken, "Iyaami". After figuring out how to properly spell the word, I began researching it online. While the Internet provided great book knowledge, I was left with the unanswered question of what Iyaami meant for me. I had absolutely no idea, but I knew it had to be something important. Why else would that specific word continue to be spoken through me?

In addition to wanting to know more about the Iyaami, I was also reading a fascinating book at the time, entitled, The Magdalen Manuscript, by Tom Kenyon and Judi Sion. It's a channeled book about Mary Magdalen, in her own words, who was a high initiate of the Temple of Isis, and her tantric relationship with Yeshua ben Joseph, also known as Jesus Christ. It's a powerful story about divine union. Mary Magdalen's words were familiar to me. They resonated deeply and I needed someone to help me explore that more.

I stumbled upon the Institute of Whole Life Healing's website and clicked the Contact Us link. The rest is history as they say. Iya Osunnike responded to my inquiry. Shortly after our initial connect via email, I attended my first Igniter Weekend with Iya Osunnike and a group of women from different parts of the country. During an igniter, you are encouraged to go deep within and explore those parts of yourself that have been hidden or repressed and are in need of healing. I have been a part of the Institute ever since that first gathering.

## The Story of My Original Birth

Nine years ago, I received a priceless gift. I was shown the origins of my beginning during a regression session with Iya Osunnike and Baba ji Koleoso. Completely unaware of what to expect, I found myself in a black void. To my left and right, it was pitch black. In front of and behind me, it was pitch black. Beneath me was pitch black. I was not aware of my body; there was simply a sense of being. I was strangely calm in this thick ebony...comfortable in the dark. As I continued taking in the darkness that surrounded me, I began to wonder. Is there something more to this space, this place, wherever, this place was? And, then I looked up and I saw it! Swirls of purples and blues dotted with billions of points of light...stars, they were! I was staring into the cosmos and in a flash, I was pulled up and out of the blackness and I was a part of the universe moving with the stars. I was a star, a beautiful point of light.

No matter how hard Iya tried to take me back to being birthed through my Earthly mother, I kept returning to the stars. I was not born moving down through the birth canal of my physical mother. I was birthed rising up through the cosmic womb of the Great Mother.

At a very young age, around 7, I began to experience a knowing. I would know things before they occurred. I would see things I dare not mention to any other. At age 10, while sitting in Sunday school, I decided that I was not any less close to God than the man in the pulpit. In addition, I knew I had a direct line to God; no middleman needed. From that point on, on a subconscious level, I believe my human self began the journey of remembrance. The spark was ignited!

Through great trial and tribulation, ridicule and criticism, and many successes, I began to accept my sacred gifts; though, my spiritual calling was not clear to me.

During the same regression session, I was shown symbols written in light. Over the years, I have come to understand I was being shown the cosmic language of light. This language is frequency-based and not interpreted by the mind but instead by the universal heart.

During this trip back down memory lane, I began to realize that I was being trained for the spiritual and energetic work that needed to be done in Philly.

# Wholeness

The people of Ancient Kemet believed the role of the female was equally as significant as that of the male. All male deities have female counterparts of equal importance. They believed in the balance of male and female energies in both the universe and in human society.

Wholeness is found when we have forgiven ourselves and others and by uniting the God and Goddess within. As I work to integrate and balance the masculine Shango and feminine Oshun energies within myself, I am teaching others how to do the same. It is said, "We teach that which we must learn." I am a teacher and a student reflecting back to humanity the divine expression of the Creator/Creatrix and humanity reflects the same back to me. I am seeing myself in Philly, in the people, places and things here. There is no separation. I am reflecting back to Philly their own light. Although, some cannot see it just yet for the darkness, it is bright and luminous. We are all lights in this vast universe.

# The Betrayal

I had a profound experience during a channeling session about five years ago. Typically, I will spontaneously begin to speak another language, which I am unable to interpret. During this session, I was able to capture the word, Adesuwa. I discovered it is actually an African name. Adesuwa was a beautiful princess and the daughter of Ezomo N'Uzebu of the ancient Benin kingdom during the reign of Oba Akengbuda to whom she was betrothed in 1752. Out of the billions of names in the world, Adesuwa, which I had never heard before, came through my lips. Coincidence? I think not.

In short, Adesuwa was abducted by a visiting chief from Oboro who was in awe of her beauty. Her abductor intended to have her as one of many in his harem. When Adesuwa protested and insulted this chief in front of his subordinates, he beheaded her without hesitation. This set into motion a civil war between Benin and Oboro that ended with Benin as the victor.

My mouth dropped open discovering this piece of African history and, more so, over how it came to me. Suspecting a connection, I worked with Iya Osunnike and learned I carried, in my womb over lifetimes, this energy of rage over that injustice. It would surface during the early stages of my spiritual development when channeling an energy by the name of Oni. When she arrived, it was always through this deep wailing of pain and anger...unrestrained and raw. That energy coupled with my own earthly experiences of violence, betrayal, and pain at the hands of men made for a very heavy load to carry!

# Call To Action

Following my return to Philly, as I slept in my cave-like room, I experienced an epiphany in the form of an intense dream. Upon awakening from the dream, I was given a task by spirit. My incredulous reply to the request, you want me to do what? Write what? To whom? That's a tall order!, I whispered, as the tears rolled down my cheeks.

If we are to heal, we must first be able to forgive. Forgiveness is not always easy. We must peel back many layers to get to the core of our wounds. Sometimes, we do not even realize how deeply we are hurting until we go deep within ourselves and pull up stuff long forgotten. The shadow darkness can sometimes keep us from our light, especially when we do not know the shadow is there. God/Goddess knows I have had my challenges in the forgiveness department. I would often ask myself, how can I forgive the heinous acts of others that have caused death, destruction and despair?

It took me many years to truly understand forgiveness is not for the other person, it is for me. Nelson Mandela said, "Not forgiving someone is like drinking poison and expecting the other person to die." It is imperative we do the inner work and release what is holding us prisoner. Without that work, we will not grow and evolve. I often hear Baba ji say, "On your journey, be gentle with yourself." It is imperative to remember this as well! We can go kicking and screaming, while being dragged, or we can surrender and let go and embrace those moments that come with grace and ease.

Recognizing that everything we experience is in divine order, though we may not recognize it at the time, is key. The Law of Resonance is based on the scientific understanding that everything in the universe is made up of energy and vibrates at a specific frequency. This means as energetic beings, we attract into our lives what is resonating at the same frequency as we are. When we truly understand this truth, we can begin to raise our vibration through healing and forgiveness.

For millennia, masculine energy has ruled this planet creating a cosmic imbalance in the world. If we are to heal as a planet, the God/Goddess energies must be in balance. In light of all that the hood was teaching me, and the healing I had done within myself to cleanse and purify residual energies left from lifetimes of trauma both within and outside of the hood, I was guided to write an open letter of forgiveness to the men on behalf of the Sacred Feminine. This letter is the preamble to the healing spiritual and energetic work I have come to do here in Philly.

# Open Letter of Forgiveness

From the Cosmic Womb of darkness, all life is created.

From a healed place representing the Sacred Feminine, we write this open letter of forgiveness to those men who do not recognize their Divine Masculine. For in truth, it was you who facilitated our awakening by forcing us to stand up for ourselves and step into our own power in a balanced way. It was you who forced us to determine what is acceptable and what is not. It was you who forced us to determine our own worth and value. In the wise words of Bashar, "I am who I am and that is enough." We take responsibility for the part we have played in this imbalance. We are perfectly imperfect, and we are enough.

On behalf of the Sacred Feminine and from the Cosmic Womb of darkness, we forgive you, the egocentric men, for the atrocities against men, women, and children in your pursuit of power, control, and money. With compassion, we recognize you do not see the world with your universal heart.

On behalf of the Sacred Feminine and from the Cosmic Womb of darkness, we forgive you, the warmongers, for the death, destruction, and bloodshed you have brought upon humanity. With compassion, we recognize you do not see that as you kill others, you are killing yourselves, as we are all divine reflections of one another and birthed from the same Source.

On behalf of the Sacred Feminine and from the Cosmic Womb of darkness, we forgive you, the pimps and rapists for desecrating and devaluing our sacred temples, our bodies, as a means of currency and control for you. With compassion, we recognize you do not see that for every woman you desecrate and devalue, you desecrate and devalue all women, including your great-grandmothers, grandmothers, mothers, and daughters.

On behalf of the Sacred Feminine and from the Cosmic Womb of darkness, we forgive you, the money hungry men, for the rape of Gaia, our Mother Earth, of her precious resources, desecration of her lands and pollution of her waters. With compassion, we recognize you do not see Mother Earth as a living and conscious being, and that we are children within her the womb. As Mother Earth suffers, we all suffer.

On behalf of the Sacred Feminine and from the Cosmic Womb of darkness, we forgive you, the misogynistic men, for your hate of women and constant attack on our feminine essence. With compassion, we recognize you do not see that without us, you would not be.

On behalf of the Sacred Feminine, and from the Cosmic Womb of darkness to those men who are broken, beat down, and emasculated, we recognize how heavy your hearts are given all you have been through. We know you are hurting and are not allowed to show it because you were taught that vulnerability is weakness. We know you are tired and weary and must push through, despite the challenges you face. We encourage you to look within and find those places needing healing and release. For you are gods asleep waiting to be awakened.

We hold that as all of you forgive yourselves and others, you will ascend to the highest expression of who you are as the Divine Masculine.

Trust in your divine counterpart, the Sacred Feminine. We see your *light*. We are here to *nurture* you. We are here to assist in *healing* you if you let us. We need your *strength*. We need your *protection*. We need your *love*.

From the Cosmic Womb of darkness, we, the Sacred Feminine, now bring forth *luminous light*.

From the Cosmic Womb of darkness, we, the Sacred Feminine, now bring forth *Unconditional Divine Love*.

From the Cosmic Womb of darkness, we, the Sacred Feminine, now bring forth *peace*.

From the Cosmic Womb of darkness, we, the Sacred Feminine, now bring forth *harmony*.

From the Cosmic Womb of darkness, we, the Sacred Feminine, now bring forth restored *balance* between *God/Goddess*.

From the Sacred Feminine, we also ask that the brothers forgive the brothers for not standing up or showing up when called or needed and for not being the beacons of light for those younger brothers who looked up to you.

Lastly, on behalf of the Sacred Feminine and from the Cosmic Womb of darkness, we thank the Divine Masculine for taking responsibility and asking forgiveness for their part in this imbalance. To experience their request firsthand, I invite you to learn more about Iseluleko Ma'at El 0 and his The Divine Man: Men's Self-Mastery Program at: www.iseluleko.com

# Illumination

The H.O.O.D. has so beautifully reminded me of the following:

---

I am a phenomenal womb (man)

I am committed to living my truth

I recognize my power and will continue cultivating it

I am raw, wild and beautiful

I will never again allow others to determine my value

I will honor my sacred womb and teach other women how to do the same

I am my mother's mothers' daughter, and they are beyond definition

I have divine and cosmic gifts to share with humanity

I am committed to seeing, feeling and knowing God/Goddess in all things

I am uniquely me

---

My return to Philly has shown me the inter-generational trauma is tied to the imbalance between the masculine and feminine energies. It is my calling to assist in energetically cleansing, lifting and elevating through the reconsecration of what was devalued, dehumanized and destroyed here in Philly. Our Ancestors are calling for this and it will be done with the support of others in the Philadelphia community.

For those reading these words, know that you too are illuminated and cosmic beings. You are divine reflections of the one source known by many names. Take your experiences and circumstances and look beyond the obvious. Find the lessons and messages and guidance in everything you do, see and feel. Peeling back the layers and digging deep within, your true self will be revealed.

My years at the Institute helped me to truly see who I am and what I bring to the world. I am still a student at the Institute. I believe that we never stop learning and growing. Evolving takes lifetimes and is never-ending. Trust in your journey and remain open to receive what is needed for your own illumination and ascension.

# Priestess AyoDeji

Lisa "AyoDeji" Allen began her spiritual journey of knowing at a very young age. Following a paranormal experience in 1996, she awakened to her gift as a channel.

AyoDeji was initiated as a Yoruba priestess of Shango in 2003. Guided by Spirit, she connected with the Institute of Whole Life Healing and was initiated as a priestess of Oshun in 2013.

With her B.A. in English, Ayo Deji often supports her community. A natural empath, she works with the energies associated with the Egyptian lion-headed goddess Sekhmet.

Also known as Inara, ray of light, she is passionate about humanity's connection to the cosmos and all things mystical. Her favorite spiritual tools include tarot, crystals, and numerology. She has also been recently called to create beaded jewelry designed by Spirit.

If you are interested in spiritual reading or custom jewelry, she may be reached via email at: sirian1111@gmail.com.

# Surrendering to a Higher Spiritual Truth
## Phyllis Douglass (Vox Angelus)

People are being guided to go inward on the cusp of an incredible time in our history, where we are being given an opportunity to rise up out of an old and outdated paradigm, to make individual, communal and societal shifts.

People are beginning to awaken to an inner calling—a divine pull or feeling-- that there is something missing within their lives.

Are you sensing there is something more for you to discover, but you don't know what it is?

In this time of rapid spiritual awakening through experience, self-discovery, and revelation, you may have found yourself feeling that what you are seeking seems inaccessible. You may feel like you are doing something wrong or are even unworthy of attaining your desire.

Nothing could be further from the truth!

The reason many people cannot find what they are seeking, or wishing to create in their lives, simplistically comes down to frequency, resonance, and vibration. All aspects of who we are—physical, emotional, mental, spiritual and energetic--must be a frequency match, or in vibrational alignment with our desires.

In my sessions, focused on creating alignment through the shifting of frequency and vibration, I've met and worked with people throughout the world who share this same experience. They've begun to feel restless and unfulfilled. They become seekers within the world, looking for a seemingly elusive answer, to their desire to be more positively fueled within their lives.

However, what people are truly seeking has never been accessible within the external world. It can only be found when we seek the path inward, which when traveled reveals the truth of who we are, as individuations of Infinite Source God in physical form. When we can accept our own divinity and allow this truth to be expressed within our lives, everything becomes open and available to us.

In my chapter, I share a bit about my lifelong connection and relationship with Elohim, the importance of attuning our resonant frequency, and how the understanding and acceptance of a single truth will serve to alter your life trajectory.

All of my sessions, trainings, workshops, and performative offerings are experienced in divine union with Elohim, and the presence of Angels.

My handcrafted and divinely inspired spiritual tools, which are encoded and alchemically activated by Elohim and can be found at www.alchemicalsacreds.com.

If you are interested in receiving guidance from myself and Elohim, and are open to making a transformational shift within your life, please connect with me @ www.PhyllisDouglass.com.


*I AM in stillness*
*Silence that is deafening*
*Takes away my breath.*

*I SEE the pathway*
*Beckoning me through the dark*
*As my eyes adjust.*

*I HEAR many thoughts*
*None of which are worth thinking*
*As I shift my mind.*

*I make a new choice*
*To transcend the older ways*
*And become as ONE.*

I was born on the sixth day of August, 1961. Transported via a bright, blue flash of lightning through an electromagnetic energy matrix, and planted within a protective container made up of flesh, blood, bone and sinew.

Fully ensouled within my mother's womb, this then tiny bundle of joy had an, "Oh, shit!" moment. And I wondered what had motivated me to acquiesce when asked to enter another physical life experience!

Moments prior, I had been in conversation with beings that did not exist within the physical world, discussing the spiritual climate on our sentient planet Earth and my pending mission. In those moments, I did not exist within the physical world.

There was a moment of regret, and then a subsequent loss of memory, as I made my way down the birth canal into a brightly lit and mysterious world.

My mission in this lifetime is to assist in guiding the awakening and enlightenment of humanity to a higher level of conscious awareness of their true Godself. When we can acknowledge and accept that we are an individuation of God experiencing a physical life, we begin to reawaken to the inner spark of divinity residing within each of us.

I was approached and given the opportunity to come back into a physical form to accomplish a specific directive, to take on the role of a Holy Messenger. Though within my work I am defined as a healer and spiritual teacher, what I reveal through my sessions, workshops, and retreats, is your true nature is that of a penetrating and powerful force of creative expression within the realm of matter.

My primary instrument of transformation comes through the use of my voice as a direct and embodied conduit for the consciousness of Elohim.

Elohim is essentially how I communicate with God. It is the highest consciousness to intervene and interact with humanity as we awaken to our true nature, evolve individually and as a collective, and assist our process of Ascension. Elohim is the creator and architect of our existence and one of the original seeds of human consciousness.

Though the term is not to my liking, I am a Channel for nonphysical beings residing within dimensions and planes of existence, outside of our own, and at times, seemingly, well beyond what some may term our limited level of understanding.

The truth is we are not limited by anything other than the limitations we have placed upon ourselves out of fear and misguided, incorrect or adopted beliefs.

Everyone who incarnates into physical life is on a specific mission to learn and experience the desires of the Soul. Some pursuits may appear bigger and more apparent than others, as you stand witness to an experience outside of your own. However, please know that the worth of each human beings' experience is equally weighted towards the totality of the collective human experience.

Everyone's life story is different. Each page of our story is written from the moment of our birth into this world to the moment we take our final exhale and transition out of our present physical form. From the first hour of life, we begin to learn and experience. Life is meant to be experience after experience after experience, filling the hyphen between our birthdate and our so-called death. Our experiences from an early age are molded by our parents, family members, caretakers, teachers, clergy, and everyone we meet and engage with--and even those we watch from afar. We learn from any experience, even when we lack the original context, because in some way, it spoke to us on a deeper level that needs no justification.

We are bombarded by news programs, reality shows, political and social agendas. And from all of this and more, we develop or adopt systems of belief, morals and values, and differing ways of being to survive within the world. We are programmed to be and act in a certain way that others deem appropriate. However, when we live our lives based upon other peoples' desires and expectations about what our life should look like, there comes a point of emptiness or unfulfillment because our heart and spirit are not being properly fueled.

As everything in the universe is sacredly designed through sound, frequency, resonance and vibration, this presents on a soul level as a misalignment that begins to cause increasing levels of dis-ease within our lives. The longer we deviate from our Soul's true path and purpose, the more difficult life, seemingly, becomes. And it feels like we are trying to swim upstream against a mighty current.

This is a sure sign that we are traveling in the wrong direction. It is our intuition and higher guidance telling us that what we are doing, or the path we are presently traveling, is not in alignment with who we are meant to become.

Our first reason for desiring to exist in a human form is to experience all aspects of living a physical life that fulfills our desire to learn from and appreciate the life we are leading.

Our second reason is to live a revelatory life that ultimately reveals our true and divine nature. When we choose to embrace our divinity and allow this truth to permeate and direct every aspect of our lives--physically, emotionally, mentally, spiritually, and energetically, the more aligned and centered we are able to become and the more capacity we have to approach our lives from the perspective of our higher, unlimited self.

In my work, I share tools and resources with my clients and students from my own life experience, and the wisdom of Elohim, to help them access the incredible power we each have within to create the life we desire.

We all have this ability. How?

The past and the future do not exist in the present moment. Within the present moment, the past no longer exists, unless we've declined to liberate or detach ourselves emotionally from our past experiences. And the future has yet to be determined. It is simply unlimited potentiality.

If we wish to transform our lives, we must be in vibrational alignment, through our thoughts and actions in the present moment, with the future we desire to create.

Simplistically speaking, our present vibration magnetizes the circumstances, experiences, and relationships needed to maintain our present experience. If you don't like what you see, you need to change your vibrational frequency to alter your trajectory.

This is essentially the law of attraction. Reality is such that you will not see nor experience that which you are not a vibrational match for. This is the only thing that truly stops us from creating what we desire.

Many people never venture outside of the uncompromising paradigms, belief structures, and programming of their childhood. However, many more are awakening and stepping out from under the umbrella and allowing the reality of life to rain down upon them creating clarity and a forever deepening curiosity for something new.

Often there is an overwhelming feeling that there is much more to life than what we have been seeing and engaging with. Curiosity is a game changer and it is the master key that opens many new doors.

Our self-realizations and discoveries are what start the ball rolling for our spiritual awakening and ascension, but in order for this to happen, we have to discard our old beliefs that no longer ring true.

Throughout all of this, whether we choose to recognize it or not, the Infinite Source, which I call God, is continually speaking and working as and through us, within our available energetic capacity in each moment. We may not be listening, nor responding to, God's thusly one-sided dialogue.

This is the calling you may sense within you that there is so much more available to you. This is the divine pull that suddenly makes you realize it's time to move on from a job or a relationship because you are feeling unfulfilled or sensing there is something else you're supposed to be doing with your life. Our Higher Self is reminding us that we are here to fulfill our soul's journey and we are out of alignment.

This is God calling us home to ourselves!

Through my spiritual offerings and teachings, I help you to recognize and honor this truth. I help you to align with your Soul's path and purpose to become the person you are meant to be by providing the Access Points needed to explore, experience, and discover who you truly are. Working with Elohim, we scan your past, present, and future to reveal and resolve the influences in your life that are keeping you from moving forward. We provide frequency adjustments through direct alchemical transmission to bring you back into alignment.

When I was four years old, I was in Sunday School in the United Methodist Church and given my first child bible. I was fascinated with the beautiful and colorful pictures throughout, and this was the first time I'd heard about Angels. There was a picture of a glorious Angel in red robes with huge white wings and a golden halo hung in the air above its head.

From that day forward, I understood the nonphysical beings, who have surrounded me since as early as I can remember, to be Angels. Sometimes, they were biblically classic in appearance and other times, they took on a human form. As I became older and more familiar with their frequencies, the Angels' need to show physical form diminished, as I was able to recognize their presence without the need to see them physically. Even in human form, I knew them by their energy signature. Throughout my life, the Angels have served as my friends, teachers, guides and protectors. Frankly, I've never questioned my relationship with them. They have always been by my side or their presence easily accessible through focused intention.

I have always implicitly trusted them and had continued faith in God despite adversity and challenge. No matter what experiences I have created within my life, my only stumbling point has been a lack of trust in myself. And in challenging times and circumstances, the Angels remind me to trust and maintain my faith.

"They are only experiences after all and not defining moments reflective of the truth of who you are. They are learnings that allow you to progress forward on your journey with an accumulation of knowledge and wisdom that serves to direct your path," the Angels would advise.

Their continued presence and guidance illuminated a, sometimes, tumultuous path forward at certain points in my life. As the years passed, I recognized each experience as a necessary teaching or dissemination of ancient wisdom needed to fuel my work, spiritual unfoldment and life mission. The truth is you cannot lead the way by example or share effectively with others, if you have not experienced firsthand what you are teaching or sharing.

With experience comes an irreplaceable depth of knowledge, understanding and courage. Direct experience also lays down a tried-and-true map for others to follow allowing them to gain similar results that stand the test of time.

When I was in my mid-30s, I was in prayer envisioning the visage of Jesus as portrayed in biblical texts. The Angels came to me and stated that I needed to place my focus upon the flesh of his feet and worn leather sandals. In essence to allow myself to walk in his shoes.

When I pushed back asking why, they told me it was time to reflect upon the truth of his humanity versus an idyllic misrepresentation introduced in scriptures and biblical stories. They quoted phrases from the Bible and Gospels that were altered, removed or otherwise not presented in their full original context. The key thing they wished for me to understand is Jesus was a human man who knew his Father. He understood and fully acknowledged his divine nature as an individuation of God in a physical form and expressing as God out into the world as a Healer and Prophet.

He was in direct relationship and communion with God, the Father. This is what he shared in his teachings.

This understanding allowed Jesus to perform what people deemed as miraculous feats. His desire was that all men and women understand and acknowledge they are of same lineage and capability and that the essence of God fuels our Soul and expresses as and through all things in existence.

By changing my perspective and hesitantly stepping into Jesus' story detailed within scripture and other texts, I began to recognize his humanness as I attempted to be both an inward and outward reflection of his words and actions. This insight allowed me to begin to open and hone my own channel of direct communion and relationship with God from within myself.

Over a period of time, I gradually began to note how my choices and subsequent experiences had come to define who I thought I was and others assumed me to be. The task of accumulating ways to identify ourselves as something that others can recognize, appreciate, and respect has been an ingrained and gradually depreciating pathway in people's lives since childhood—including my own.

I had been restricting, becoming an extension of this infinite force of creative expression—God--because I was trying to be everything but that. God isn't the title of daughter, son, sister, brother, woman, man, mother, father, wife, husband,or your mode of employment. God isn't how much money you have or don't have in the bank.

I was beginning to understand that my relationship with God, and not in a religious sense, was the key to a happy, joyful, and balanced life of magical manifestation.

Your name, your history, where you live, your degrees and certificates, your relationships and, essentially, all of your life experiences were never meant to define you! Your true nature of being is undefinable and centered within a unified sphere of eternal completeness. Your true essence has no needs to be met other than the desire to experience life. When the physical vehicle we inhabit reaches its limitations and we release our final exhale, we bid farewell to a life well-lived and transition into our original form.

The beautiful body we leave behind is nothing but a sweet and self-honoring vessel that houses our divine force, so we can express our true selves within the physical world. Our Godself.

*I AM here right now*
*Empowered to move forward*
*On the waves of Love.*

*I have now blossomed*
*From seeds planted in the past*
*Now fueled from the Sun.*

*I now simply AM*
*Released from old storied ways*
*That captured my mind.*

*I fly on the wind*
*And this heightened perspective*
*Shows beauty and grace.*

We have come to define ourselves as other, inadequate and separate; when, in reality, we are truly same, capable, and powerful.

It was important to acknowledge and witness myself and others as no different from Jesus. We are all the sons and daughters of God. The only difference is Jesus knew, without a shadow of doubt, who and what he was in relationship to God the Father and, equally, Mother God. When we understand and accept our true nature of being and eternal essence, the veil falls away to reveal ourselves as both created and creator of our lives. We become fully present in the moment and physical life becomes a reflection of the inner Godself—our holy, eternal essence, seeking to be fully realized and expressed into the world.

We are all—each one of us—capable of spiritual mastery and quantifiable healing as witnessed flowing as and through Jesus. In essence, we are meant to physically and spiritually walk in his shoes. We were never meant to revere the appearance and personification of Jesus engrained through religious indoctrination that maintains our separation and solidifies the false understanding that something impenetrable resides between us and God.

The force of God is the common thread woven through one's internal and external world. Serving as the point of connectivity between all things in existence, we must begin to recognize and acknowledge this essence of God as our true nature of being. This understanding is the precursor for one's spiritual and evolutionary unfoldment and allows you to experience physical life from this limitless and omnipresent perspective that is our birthright.

What I've discovered is life is about aligning with the ultimate and limitless frequency of God by recognizing our Godself within, which is always in communion with this highest force of creative expression found within all things. When we are connected in this way, we remain present in the moment with the knowing that the future will simply unfold in alignment with our higher state of being.

Acknowledgment of our Godself provides us with the dual perspective of being both created and Creator because we are God within the freedom of a physical body that gets to play this game called Life. This is the key to liberation from past restraints, conditioning and limiting beliefs.

And each experience serves as a key to discover who we are and to find our own voice.

The Angels have always told me that I must continue to trust and have faith through each of my experiences. However, there were many trying times that I held onto only the mere notion of God because I could not see God within tumultuous and traumatic experiences throughout my life. I would find myself asking Elohim why they had allowed certain things to happen. In truth, throughout all the trials and my queries to the heavens, I always felt a loving strength and presence. I cannot say I truly knew exactly what it was back then but I can now state, unequivocally, what I've felt deep within my heart all along is God.

When I was in my late 30s, the Angels came to me and stated I would no longer be able to use tools of any sort within my healing practice such as oracle cards, crystals and Reiki symbols. They stated, "The time has come that you recognize yourself as an instrument of Infinite Source and nurture your ability to communicate directly with God."

It was a scary proposition. At the time, I had a very successful and thriving healing practice that included Usui Reiki and the Pathway Prayer Method of Akashic Record Reading. In the span of a single day, everything I had learned and become proficient at went out the window! Suddenly, I found myself disconnected from the techniques I had used for years and I could recapture nothing!

I felt incapacitated understanding that I'd come to rely on external perceived sources of power. Feeling naked and inept, I felt like there was a hidden part of me I needed to retrieve and that all-knowing aspect of self that knew the way forward felt lost to me, as well, in the moment.

I was aware of my gift as a Seer and my ability to feel and manipulate energy but I'd become reliant on using oracle cards and crystals to make all of the spiritual and mystical stuff more tangible for my clients. And in a way, I believe that the use of external accoutrements psychologically relieved some of the responsibility of getting it right and not having to rely solely upon myself. Also, the oracle cards served as a spark to my intuitive self, jogging information from the ethers that I felt uncomfortable fully acknowledging I could access myself.

The Angels knew this. And because I had been ignoring their incessant prompting and guidance, I found myself in a do-or-die situation, where suddenly all of the methods I had been using to access my connection with God no longer appeared to work. When I asked them what was happening, I was told, "Just pull out your mobile phone and make a call--it's that easy."

The thing is a part of me knew of my extraordinary ability to access the divine realms and beyond. I was lacking nothing other than confidence and there were still many people, at that time within my life, who did not believe in what I was doing. No one, including myself, knew what I was fully capable of.

I'd been raised in an era where it was important to keep up outward appearances and that often meant leaning into others' expectations of what your life should look like. Many people attempted to instill fear in me to stop me from pursuing a spiritual path because it made them feel uncomfortable.

This was not only family and friends but clients as well. I'd had a thriving practice where I provided well-known practices such as Reiki. However, as soon as I began my studies of Shamanism and other energetic healing modalities, my clients began to gradually disappear. They became fearful, even at the end of a wonderful and productive session, because they didn't understand why the energy coming through felt stronger and more deeply penetrating. For many people being presented with an opportunity to change their lives, they feel more comfortable remaining within a known situation even if they are unhappy and in pain. Creating change in your life requires movement into unknown territory and shifting into unfamiliar territory can be scary.

Fear often causes people to make choices that lead nowhere keeping them stuck and complacent within the life they've created for themselves. However, being uncomfortable is a prerequisite for growth.

*All roads lead nowhere*
*Unless you can imagine*
*Where it is leading.*

*What do you desire*
*In this present moment now*
*For the future you?*

*It's time to BE that*
*Envisioning all your dreams*
*As happening now.*

*Today it begins*
*Standing at the doorway's cusp*
*Acknowledging YOU.*

*The puzzle completes*
*each piece falling into place*
*with effortless grace.*

*We are united*
*we are interconnected*
*with all that exists.*

*Open to your truth*
*and your adventurous soul*
*as we are all ONE.*

I've never liked the word, Healer. I consider myself to be a facilitator of healing helping my clients access their body's own innate healing wisdom and intelligence. You are the true healer.

We know that our mindset can heal the body as well as through the release of trauma and other intense emotional circumstances that were creating energetic distortion and blockages. I have seen firsthand in session cancerous tumors melt away or bruises from previous accidents or abuse spontaneously reoccur on the body as the body unwinds and releases the unresolved emotional impact of past circumstances.

Most people would call these occurrences miracles. Are they really?

What I began to realize is the body's innate intelligence goes largely untapped and human beings are so much more powerful and capable of creating these so-called miracles than they believe are possible. It all comes down to intention, trust and belief.

Over the years, my clients have often been my biggest teachers, Godsent to serve as a catalyst for my personal growth and evolution. My point of reentry into a new level of healing along with a very real change of mindset came when a new client came in for a session.

I sat at the head of the table realizing I had no clue what to do or where to begin!

An Angel came forward and asked, "Are you ready to surrender all of what you think you know, all of who you believe yourself to be, and to directly communicate with God?"

I said, "Yes."

"Then place your hands upon their shoulders and open yourself to God. Allow yourself to BE the work versus doing the work."

I felt a compassionate nudge and laid my hands upon my client's shoulders. And I remember saying, "Okay God, do your thing. I'm just going to sit back and witness because I don't know what else to do other than to serve as your instrument."

This is when the powerful magic of stepping fully into my power and spiritual alignment began to flow through, as a divine, transformative, and unstoppable force. There was truly nothing to do other than to hold a simple intention in a state of trust and faith in a higher power.

And I learned trust in the invisible and intangible must be extended to Self, the biggest component to our evolutionary process is to trust ourselves first and foremost.

I surrendered and began to simply allow. When my mind got in the way, I could immediately feel the misalignment and return to a higher state of awareness and deep observation.

I have now become a teacher without a specific curriculum. Pure and original teachings are based upon those who are present to receive. Therefore, what I share are tools or methods for individual evolutionary discovery, growth, development and subsequent outward expression of one's truth, gifts, and power.

Each of us has a different journey and differing infrastructures that guide our path forward. What you share with another person always serves as a key that will either unlock or lock a door, whether it's through acceptance or rejection of the information. Either way, one accepts or rejects the information that is received based upon their beliefs and desires in the moment. And it can change.

The Angels shared that a true teacher does not teach what they were taught. They teach an amalgamation of the teachings that positively served them in finding their own path in a way that is aligned with their own medicine and magic in service to others. They teach through their own experiences, successes and failures. You are the only one who can do what you do in the way that you do it.

Gradually, I began receiving a new level of clientele who were more informed, adventurous, and pursuing a spiritual path. And the level of excitement stirred the fires within me to continue doing what I was doing without question. I began to allow curiosity and excitement to be my guide.

Throughout the years, I have witnessed many miraculous things occur for both myself and others. One day, Archangel Gabriel appeared and asked, "What do you think is still holding you back from truly believing?"

It was a simple question that caught me off guard.

I've witnessed fantastical things that have left me breathless and in awe and wonder and yet I could feel something within my heart that bordered on doubt. What occurred to me in that moment is that maybe the only reason I chose to believe any of it was because, if I didn't, I would be placed in a padded room wrapped in a white straight jacket.

Somewhere an Angel rolled their eyes and groaned. They say they do not do that but I'm not so sure Angels have dealt with the likes of me before... Though I am quite hardheaded, I've followed their guidance my entire life, no matter what. I'm somewhat of a conundrum driven by a higher internal force that is loving and that I trust beyond all else: the voice of God.

I'm going to interject here with a brief recounting of one of these miracles.

When I was attending graduate school at California Institute of the Arts, I happily bounded off to visit a friend who lived in Chouinard Hall. I mention this because in order to get there I had to walk down two lengthy flights of cement stairs. As I approached the top stair, I took what must have been a grave misstep that would have most probably taken my life. As I stepped into thin air, I was suddenly surrounded by a prickly, electrical, bright blue sphere of light. In a space of no time, my next step was at the very bottom, as the sphere dissolved into thin air.

I was in a state of shock and wonder and a bit of fear. There was no possible way to discount what had just happened, so I turned to look up the stairs and yelled, "Thank you!" I then ran into the building like I was being followed by banshees.

The Angels had saved my life. Though it was the first, it was not the last time they've kept me out of harm's way.

I believe that our quick disbelief stems from fear that we as God, suddenly have to take on a great deal of responsibility within our lives. You have to accept that you are responsible for all of your creations—not just the good ones. You don't have anyone to potentially blame any longer, when things don't go the way you planned. You can give into others' beliefs and travel along with them, but if you end up in a place you didn't desire to be, it is still your fault for following them in the first place.

We have freewill, which means we have choices.

What I began to realize is when I let go of the invalid beliefs and focused on the truth of my existence and ability to communicate directly with God through Self, my life began to flow unceasingly forward. If there were obstacles that came up, I was magically provided with the tools or resources needed to move past them.

The Angels provided me with a technique to instantly connect with God that references back to their comment about connecting with God is as easy as placing a phone call.

# The Mobile Phone Technique:

First close your eyes and take a few inhalations through the nose and exhale through the mouth. Allow external distractions to drop away.

Envision an iPhone cord (or any other model phone cord) spiraling upwards towards an outlet an arms-length above your head. Visualize plugging the charging adapter into the outlet. Then follow the cord downwards to the lightening adapter or USB-C and plug this opposite end into a slot on the crown of your head. Make your call.

This method works magically for me. No matter where I am, even if there is a lot of noise and distraction, I can easily make the connection.

I was so in awe of the simplicity!

The Angels often reiterate, "Humankind loves to muddy up the waters when God has made things expressly simple. You have the means to connect through intention and speak directly with God and the higher forces of expression, without training, certificates or the permission of a self-appointed go-between, such as a priest, pastor or guru."

Take all that you have learned with a grain of salt. Each experience with a spiritual and energetic methodology or teaching serves only as a key opening doors throughout your spiritual development. Teachings you receive are not meant to mold you into a version of the teacher. They are meant to awaken your own intuition, gifts, and insightfulness. They are meant to allow the progression and unfolding of your own spiritual path, not the adoption of a path meant for another. Take only what resonates and offers you an aha perspective of your current and ever fluctuating landscape and leave everything else behind.

*Stand by who you are*
*The world will then follow you*
*And dreams will come true.*

*The world cannot know*
*The truth of who you are not*
*If you are truthful.*

*Kernels of knowledge*
*Are few and far in between*
*When minds remain closed.*

*Venture forward now*
*A child of God in power*
*Breaks all barriers.*

Be it a specific energy technique or other alternative modality, just like a piece of clothing, you are going to wear it differently. It's never going to look the same as it does on another person. We travel through life trying things on for size and surreptitiously checking the mirror to see how it looks on us.

How's the fit? The color? Do the seams line up correctly?

I have decidedly jumped off the path of forever seeking because when you are constantly searching for something, you tend to walk by the open doorways meant for you, as if you are wearing blinders.

This is true for any path you may embark upon that leads to a desired goal. There must be a balance point somewhere between seeking and, actually, finding what it is you are looking for. That's what shores up your foundation -- finding those points of balance where the stones lie on top of each other and are not in danger of toppling over. You have to know when you have reached a plateau where you feel comfortable staying for a time.

When someone climbs Mt. Everest, they don't summit in a day. They stop in key areas to acclimate themselves with their surrounding environment preparing to reach the next plateau.

Our path up the mountain isn't received from a teacher. It is about processing and integrating the knowledge that has been laid out before you and allowing yourself to evolve to the next step. The next level comes from within you.

This has been my process of spiritual evolution, which has allowed me to recognize, acknowledge and honor the truth of my existence—regardless of what others think, say, or do that may be contrary. I teach my students and clients that your power resides within your uniqueness and personal approach derived from your toolbox filled with only those things gathered throughout the years that serve to enhance the work you do in service to the world.

When you can honor the God-self within, the world truly becomes your playground.

When you walk in the footsteps of Jesus, your path forward becomes illuminated as if you've been given a map to follow from destination to destination.

In closing, I must circle back to Jesus.

Several years ago, the matter of protection kept coming up. Every form of training I pursued had a component focused on protection from taking on or receiving unwanted energies, psychic attacks, and all manner of negative things. I'd been told many times from different people that I was too open and that I needed to dim my light, so as not to attract negative entities.

I had effectively bought into it as a necessity and means of continuing the work I was doing. Then during my first Stargate Experience in Mt. Shasta, Jesus came to me in a meditation.

He stood before me in a beautiful, biblical sense that I recognized, and my first instinct was I wanted to hug him. He told me, "I have come to teach you to expand your Light," and he demonstrated how to do it.

I tried; I really did. But I must have looked, more so, like I was constipated in my efforts and nothing happened.

Jesus said, "No. Allow your radiance. Expand your Light like this," as he spread his hands away from his belly while making a puffing sound for effect, and a force of bright energy like a gale of wind almost bowled me over.

Without stopping to think about the absurdity of the experience, I did exactly what he had done with intention, blowing a puff of air from my mouth whilst envisioning being radiant. And a funny thing happened, I accomplished exactly what Jesus had done!

He told me that my radiance and connection with God was my only needed protection. And that the feeling that one needs protection serves as a distraction, diminishes one's power, and is a self-fulfilling prophecy. Aligning with your true divine nature circumvents the need for fear.

That was a lot to take in as I hugged Jesus before he vanished into thin air.

I practiced this and dispensed with all forms of protection I had previously learned. It was a bit scary in certain circumstances, but as always, I held deep trust and faith. And I found that it, actually, provided me more freedom and allowed for more expansiveness and elevation in my work.

What solidified this sense of sovereignty was a Brujeria Workshop taught by my longtime teacher and benefactor that the Angels told me to attend. I was still very nervous when it came to the talk of witchcraft at the time because in my life it had held negative connotations. However, I dutifully attended and found it to be a fascinating experience filled with information that felt unexpectedly and greatly aligned.

The kicker came with being required to complete a final exercise. We were directed outside and our teacher stated that he was going to draw white circles for each of us to stand in. He taught us a magical action and word to ward off negative entities and said that once we were all in our circles, he would summon them to approach us. When we felt their approach, we were instructed to ward them off.

I was the second person to step into a circle and, as the moments passed, my anxiety increased. I was sitting on the ground and called to the Angels stating I had no idea what to do. What he had taught us felt out of alignment.

The Angels said, "Phyllis, be who you are and do what you do."

So, I stood up and did what Jesus had taught me. I became radiant.

I waited and waited for something to happen as I heard others warding off the negative entities, as they approached. At one point, I noticed my teacher staring at me from across the way. He stood there for quite some time looking at me then continued to walk.

He announced the completion of the exercise and we reconvened indoors to discuss our experience.

I was totally befuddled because I had not had the same experience as others and tentatively raised my hand to ask my question.

"Nothing happened; did I do something wrong?" Somewhere an Angel was rolling their eyes again.

He looked at me quizzically for a moment and then replied, "Phyllis, you did everything right. You cast your sphere of energy so wide that the people who fell within it had no experience either. Where I was standing and watching you at the palpable edge of your sphere, the negative entities could not penetrate your Light!"

That was the moment I consciously surrendered to the higher truth I'd been silently cherishing and holding close to my heart, since I was a little girl. "I am God.", she whispered from deep within the mature and experienced woman she's become. My life began to unfold as a beautiful work of Art.

If you are wanting to discover and clear what is keeping you from moving forward in your own life, consider scheduling a potently and sacredly designed Session or Group Transmission with myself and Elohim.

In closing, I would like to express how grateful I am to have been asked to participate in the Institute of Whole Life Healing's book. I had the extraordinary opportunity to perform and speak at the Institute's, Annual Great Mother Honoring and Celebration in 2022. I feel that their mission, and the many offerings in service to those desiring to reconnect with their life purpose, original greatness and divinity, are greatly in resonance with my spiritual calling and work as a Sacred Spiritual Light Leader.

# Phyllis G. Douglass, a.k.a. Vox Angelus

Phyllis G. Douglass, a.k.a. Vox Angelus, is a visionary Author, Speaker, Multidimensional Sound Artist, Spiritual Healer, and direct and embodied conduit for the consciousness of Elohim. Elohim refers to her as a Transcendent Bridge, capable of facilitating states of awareness and consciousness, above and beyond the range of normal or merely physical human experience.

When Phyllis sings, her voice becomes an intelligent stream of consciousness, embedded with encoded frequencies, Light Language, and sound signatures of sacred design from the heavenly realms. She is renowned as an illuminating, healing, and transformational force, transcending all geographical, linguistic, and cultural boundaries through her unique and evolutionary Vocal Alchemy Transmissions, workshops, and private sessions with the Angels.

Connect with Phyllis for more information, private sessions, alchemy music, and event bookings at:
www.PhyllisDouglass.com

# From Heaven to Love on Earth

## Mariyamah OloMidara Hill-Sanna

Allow me to introduce myself as Queen Mother Mariyamah Olomidara Hill-Sanna a unique frequency of Sacred Spiritual Light Leadership. You see, somehow and someway from my conscious beginning when I did not have a given name or title I knew myself.

Every human being has a unique connection to our higher universal realms because yes, we are individuals, yet we are ONE. When you were born, you breathed into this earth realm your own vibrational frequency; you also brought with you your ancestral vibrational frequency. Unfortunately, during our earthly journey we often forget not only our uniqueness, we forget our oneness, and our interconnectedness.

As I share my chapter with you, know that it has been a long, challenging, yet beneficial heavenly and earthly journey. However, every conscious breath I take keeps me in alignment with my vibrational frequency and life's purpose. As you delve into the chapter see what resonates with your vibration and make sure to breath in whatever nuggets of wisdom I'm sharing.

I'm so grateful to know that I came into this world as a connecting bridge from heaven to earth to restore light and love to those who have become broken and disconnected to their higher knowing. Let's live in harmony and wholeness, and unite our frequencies from Africa to America and Beyond.

I came into this world with the mission to assist in remembering our true selves in complete wholeness – aka Divine Love. My assignment is to be a connecting Bridge between Heaven and Earth.

The first conscious thought just before I came from my mother's womb was talking to my supportive Egbe family. Everyone has a heavenly host family that you are with when you are in the other realms, they may be called by other names, but we assist each other as needed. I knew I still had the choice not to come but I inhaled a deep etheric breath and said OK here I go and then began sliding down a tunnel.

I remember learning to breathe here on earth. I must have been about two years old when suddenly, I discovered it was necessary to inhale and exhale (my chest was expanding and contracting). I tried not to do it, but it kept happening. I asked my mama, "Why do I have to keep doing this?"

She looked at me and said, "what are you doing?"

I said this.

She said you aren't doing anything.

I said yes, I am, I was not doing this before. Now I must do this.

She said, "Baby, you aren't doing anything but breathing."

I replied, "But I didn't do that before."

She tried to assure me I had been breathing all along. Yet, I insisted no I just started this. Well, we both had enough love and respect for each other to just let it pass.

My next remembrance was being about six years old, and my mother called me to come to her bedside and asked me to lay my hands on her head so her headache would go away. It seemed like something I had been doing in past lives but this time I thought about it, and it seemed puzzling. However, mom reassured me I had the gift of healing by just laying my hands on her. So of course, my belief was mama knew everything so she must be right. Well, I took a deep breath and laid my hands on her head and minutes later the headache was gone. Imagine that...

Moving into my adult years and learning more about our breath, I came to realize that spirit really is in the breath and moves through the breath. You can fast from water, food or anything, but you must breathe. Also, the spirit in the breath is a connector, we're really all in one Spirit. This revelation was not comfortable for me when I realized it was connecting me to people that I knew I didn't want to even be physically associated with never mind spiritually. But we are spirit having a human experience. The breath keeps the body alive, the body lives if there's breath moving in and out of the body. So, breath is spirit, or a manifestation of spirit, and we are truly one spirit like it or not.

I came into this world as a connecting bridge from heaven to earth restoring light and love where we have become broken/disconnected and I have the guidance and assistance of my Egbe/and other worldly Spiritual family. I knew I was a light being beginning with my conscious awakening in the womb of the Great Mother. It was the feeling of my pulsation/vibrational frequency. Initially I just observed the feeling and wondered what this delightful feeling was until I realized it was me awakening into my individuality. I realized that prior to my physical birth I would be coming into the world to usher forth my purpose leading the way as a being of light. My Light healer journey on this plane for over 30 years has been helping to remove painful blockages through energetically harmonizing vibrational frequencies as applicable.

## Harmonizing the Light and the Dark

My learning experience has taught me the more you know, the more you realize how little you know. That realization allowed me to expand my light. Everything comes from the warm, moist space of darkness in (The Womb of Creation, The Great Mother). My light helps illuminate your path allowing you to choose the road by which you will become the light for yourself and others. Perhaps through writing, teaching, having more patience or encouragement, maybe that's your road of a light worker and how you're bringing in the light. When light manifests that doesn't mean the darkness goes away, the darkness is still present supporting the light. And that is harmony.

## Bringing Harmony and Health into the World

I was seeking to delve deeper into my African spirituality when I came to the Institute of Whole Life Healing. Iya Osunnike and Baba Koleoso were just the right prescription for me. Their guidance was free enough where I didn't have to be a clone. But it was structured enough so that I could still learn and grow. The Institute of Whole Life Healing is simply just that, bringing in your light, and the remembrance and recognition of your whole life. In most cases, we think our everyday life and struggles for survival is our whole life and what we must do. That is an illusion, we are here to remember who we are, cleanse and purify, then once we remember we can live in alignment with OUR Truth. That is the teachings of the Institute of Whole Life Healing. This guidance helped me to grow in my Light. We came together and energy just blended.

Spirit brings to you what you need when you are open. I think that it's predestined and sometimes we go in every direction but the best one. Then life will teach you and you will eventually come to the place for your soul to grow. There is no right and there is no wrong, it's only a lesson. The Institute of Whole Life Healing is not in the process to recruit people but to let people know this is available, and this is what we do. And if it resonates with your soul's growth along your journey, then let's do this together. Because as I teach or help you, I am also teaching and helping myself to evolve. There is not really any big I or little you. We're all in this together.

My first initiation with the Institute was into the Sacred Feminine Mysteries – Passage into the Great Mother. After that initiation I stepped out to publicly begin doing my light healing work. Prior to that I took classes through the Holistic Nurses' Association to become a Certified Healing Touch Practitioner. I was amazed to learn "laying on of hands" as done in the down-home black churches was now a certifiable curriculum taught in the prestigious hospitals. I learned different techniques and unique methodologies. I later became a Certified Cranial Sacral Balancing Technician and Reiki Ase Master Teacher through Iya Osunnike. I opened my office in Cincinnati Ohio and continued to add healing modalities such as Aroma Therapy, Sound Vibrational Healing, Color Therapy and of late I do Yoni Steam Rebalancing services. My next initiation within the Institute was becoming a Priestess of the Yoruba Ifa deity Yemojah, Goddess of maternal love, caring nurturer, and sustainer of all life. And, I must say that I am happiest when I am of service helping to awaken the true spirit of love within each of us through harmony and health.

## The Calling Continued into the Next Stage of Leadership: Queen Mother

It was 2010, we the elder women in the Institute were conspiring to enstool Baba as King because he was definitely functioning in the role as a Light Leader/King. We were planning to surprise him for his birthday as part of an event that he was hosting to honor and acknowledge several Elder Wisdom Keeper men and he had no idea that we were going to be honoring him as King within our community. And we had no idea that he was going to be honoring and enstooling us as Queen mothers at the same event. In many African and indigenous cultures, the powerful role of Queen Mother/s is seen as the traditional King-maker, and her wisdom is a major contributing factor to the success of the Kings leadership within the community as they sit as his primary council. As the Institute's Queen Mothers, we took an oath to devote our Wisdom Keeper abilities to provide formal counsel to our Priest King. We also committed ourselves to the following local and global areas of concern which include Whole Life Healing for women, children, men, families and community, our Environment/Mother Earth, and Ancestral and indigenous cultural remembrance and reverence.

# Some of What I've Learned Along this Path as a Light Worker and Healer

This journey is really about love. And that love is not a punk love. That love is strong powerful love that walks with wisdom. Love is spirit. Joy is spirit. Wisdom is Spirit. We are Spirit with the responsibility of Choice. Learning to choose wisely and to hold oneself accountable. Another thing that I learned through my training in Healing touch, is that I'm a vessel, and it's not about me. If I'm clearing someone's blockages, I cannot want them to heal so much that I'm forcing it from my will by pulling or drawing polluted energy to myself. I have to be in a state of neutrality and allow them to be wherever they are in their journey. You as the client must choose your process and progress. I can't want more for you than you want for yourself.

# Home To Mama Africa

I am living in Ghana, West Africa. My home is in the village of Emissano near the Gulf of Guinea almost at the center of the world. The Emissi River flows in front of my home as she also flows parallel to the Atlantic Ocean. It really feels like sacred space.

One of the names given to me by Baba Koleoso is "Mother of Two Waters" now here I am. The first-time I visited Mama Africa was about 2010 and I knew then I would build a healing space where people can come and reconnect with their Divinity. I wanted to be that connector bridge. I believe everyone needs to let their feet touch the soil of their ancestors at least one time. Mama Africa is the birthplace of all humanity. It was my desire to be a familiar face so people will feel comfortable returning to a strange but familiar land. I named this space Harmony and Health Sanctuary.

Everything in this dimension has a vibrational frequency. When you were born, you brought your own vibrational frequency, but you also brought with you your ancestral vibrational frequency. Many of us relocated from our original birthplace and our frequency is altered a bit to be in alignment with the frequencies surrounding us. But at the core of your being, you will always be that divine spirit having a human experience.

I believe everybody should travel the whole world because the whole world was created for us. Each country has its unique frequency. America has her frequency; the United States has its own frequency. Turtle Island, which is the name the original people called America still has her own frequency. Now people see her as United States of America, but that was just a name given to her by the people that came and brought their thoughts, behaviors, and their energy to Turtle Island.

Mama Africa has her own special vibrational energy, and it's my belief that everyone originated from an African Woman. I feel it would be healing for you and for your ancestral line to touch this soil at least once in your lifetime. Allow yourself to be open to see what your soul can learn and what you can remember. Harmony and Health Sanctuary is a special place, a retreat, for people to be at peace. A safe space to re-member.

## I Want to Leave You with this Wisdom

When you feel something that resonates with you, just be still and listen with no preconceived judgement. Honor your truth with love. Listen to the gentle wise voice in you. Pay attention to what your feelings are expressing. Listen to your heart, your gut, and your mind. Pay attention to the stillness within, everything outside of your inner being is designed to keep you busy and tied up and attracted to the illusion. You are not to be trained by artificial intelligence. They can give you certain lessons, but you need to know the truth and analyze it as a Divine Being of choice. Keep your humanity. Be aware that it's a gift. And there are energies out there that try to pull you away - it is deliberate. Understand that, and don't be fearful or hostile. You can win these battles just by being you, respecting you, loving you. You are not a victim. You are special. You are divine. You are wonderful. You are beautiful. You are loved. You are....

# Queen Mother Mariyamah "OloMidara"

Queen Mother Mariyamah OloMidara Hill-Sanna is a naturally gifted healer, an initiated priestess within the Sacred Feminine Mysteries, Reiki Ase Master, Priestess of Yemoja in the Yoruba Tradition, and Queen Mother enstooled through the International Institute of Whole Life Healing. Queen Mother Olomidara knows that perfect health and natural healing are our birth right. Health must occur on all levels; physical, mental, emotional, and spiritual to be restored to wholeness.

Queen Mother Mariyamah Olomidara also believes that our environment plays a crucial role in one's healing. To further support her vision of wholeness and healing for humanity, she is creating the Harmony and Health Sanctuary in Ghana West Africa. This Healing & Wellness Space is located on the beach of the Emmissi River at the mouth of the Atlantic Ocean – ideal for restoration of natural healing and wellbeing; it is also a spiritual bridge which weaves together our Ancestral traditions of East with West.

# The Journey of a Sacred Spiritual Light Leader

## Marshall Omitosin Henderson Jr.

Incarnate beings on this earth may not know early in their life that they are chosen to make the world a better place or bring light into the world to elevate the planet. The being goes through the trials and tribulations of spiritual enslavement during their lifetime and then wakes up one day from the craziness on planet Earth to discover that through their innate gifts and tools, they are here to lead those lost souls into spiritual liberation.

This chapter is about helping those Souls discover their spiritual truth by looking at why they came back to the Earth as Sacred Spiritual Light Leaders. These souls know they are here to make a change on Earth but need clarification about their mission, path, and calling in life. But they are trying to understand what that looks like for them while they are here.

This chapter indicates how I enrolled as a Sacred Spiritual Light Leader by looking at the spiritual examples of my ancestral lineage, observing the illustrations of my grandparents and father giving back to the community and taking care of their family, having conversations with my spiritual teachers and taking on the spiritual responsibilities that were assigned to me by the universe and my Godparents.

At the beginning of each section, you will see Divine wisdom known as Sacred Odu from the West African Spiritual System (Ifa) out of Nigeria, which supports my journey to know how I have become a Scared spiritual light leader.

# Oyeku Ogbe

"Behold! If you get to earth do not forget Heaven; the earth is a marketplace of suffering, Heaven is your home!!

We all live in a prison on this earth, a prison without walls or concrete structures. This prison metaphysically represents human beings on this earth being programmed from the time they come out of their mother's womb throughout their journey of life and being controlled by other people's thoughts and philosophy (e.g., religion, culture, and politics) and not being able to think or seek for themselves. For thousands of years, this planet has been revolving around negative energies that have spiritually, mentally, and physically wounded the human severely. This condition is not a color, ethnic group, or political problem. It is a spiritual warfare that operates from a negative energy constantly damaging humans daily; this negative energy goes by various names: dogma, discrimination, war, famine, slavery, greed, and sex trafficking.

These are not the only negative energies that can be identified; there are more. This negative energy is so powerful and overwhelming that if you are not grounded in the positive energy of spirituality, it can take over any human soul to bring about destruction and damage to the people and the earth.

Muata Ashby writes on page 158 in his book Egyptian yoga: All evil is born out of the ignorance of the mind. Due to ignorance of our true nature, we forget we are really one with all other beings. We begin to think we are individuals (egoism) who must struggle against other individuals, and we develop a fear of death. Due to ignorance, we hurt others by acting in Evil ways. Thus, due to ignorance we commit crimes against others, the world and ourselves. Thus we become "evil doers", Devils.

Planet Earth is in a spiritual deficit, meaning that Evil outweighs Good, and we are totally out of alignment with truth, justice, enlightened balance, and good character. In the Yoruba tradition of Ifa, this is called Iwa Pele (Good character); in the Ancient Kemetic (Egypt) spiritual system, this falls in line with the Maatian Principle (righteousness, order, and balance). The question becomes who will help bring about these spiritual principles to help planet Earth restore its balance.

On our planet, we have a plethora of religious and spiritual helpers attempting to combat evil atrocities and bring the Earth back to the divine balance of righteousness. But sometimes, this comes with a price. That price is that you must become a follower of that spiritual or religious practice. If you don't follow those certain ideologies or philosophies, you may be judged as a sinner, evil, or someone who doesn't believe in God in the way that religion believes in it.

## Iwori Irosun

"There is no real Gain in wrong-doing: there is no joy nor peace from wrong-doing. The soul of the wrong-doer will continually return to earth until a good position is reached. Seek wisdom; do good; help others; increase the prosperity of the world" Thus Spoke Orunmila.

Some soul beings have incarnated back into this plane of existence to help the planet restore its balance and bring good. They are seen as Sacred Spiritual Light Leaders. These Sacred Spiritual Light Leaders are not concerned with dogmatic religions, cultural nonsense, biased philosophies and ideologies, gender, age, or race. These Sacred Spiritual Light Leaders are not worried about the overrated titles (doctor, lawyer, president, CEO, minister, priest, etc.). These Light Leaders know they are here to bring good to the earth through spiritual elevation, illumination, and ascension.

They are here to bring light to the planet and help those souls ready to break the barriers of negative energies that keep them in spiritual bondage. They work collectively with other light beings who have also come to the planet to do this work. Their job is to help humanity evolve and become spiritually liberated from other people's thoughts and beliefs. To get humans to think for themselves or, to put it in another way, to let the universe guide them and show them the door of universal initiation. The new beginning or the initial start of universal autonomy in one's life journey.

We must realize that as a soul being travels through the sacred portal of its mother's womb and incarnates on this earth, the soul being is programmed from that day on. The soul being is given a name, gender, and age. As the beings continue to walk this earth and become older, they will be indoctrinated by technology, regurgitated education, cultural garbage, belief systems, and a God/deity from a biased perspective. All these barriers will send the being down the rabbit hole of spiritual enslavement. Sacred Spiritual Light Leaders will guide and support those beings taking a spiritual excursion on "Many paths one truth" going back into the infinite portal of truth, also known as creation, with direct experience.

To be called into this role, you must let your ego (easing God out) go and let the higher power you call on divinely guide you. The Sacred Spiritual Light Leader is a title that can't be bestowed upon you. You must work for this title and avoid getting enamored with people praising you. This title is like when you read about Buddha and Jesus/Yeshua; they never called themselves those titles. They showed through their example of hard work, love, and compassion. They were not concerned about anything other than following the universe's path. Yeshua/Jesus said, "I am about my father's business."

What I didn't know about this role was that it can be very challenging, and it may look easy from the outside but the Sacred Spiritual Light Leader must be grounded and secure within himself and not bring their shit to other people. It is one of the reasons why when a person is initiated as a priest or a spiritual leader, they are asked to leave the negative energies they have accumulated at the door because it will affect the people they are trying to help. My Godfather, Baba Koleoso, would share his sage wisdom when students wanted to be a Sacred Spiritual Light Leader, i.e. (priest, get initiated, or lead people spiritually). He would sit back and look at you or laugh at you and say, "Oh, so you want to be a priest? Oh, so you want to lead people spiritually? Oh, you want to get initiated?" This deep knowledge would flow from Baba's mouth and say, "When you take on a student/godchildren or initiate people, you are taking on their karma." He shared his profound knowledge about the Sacred Spiritual Light Leader because he knew it was not easy being in this role and that sometimes it doesn't come with all the bells and whistles. He never looked at the Sacred Spiritual Light Leader negatively; he would always remind us that it is a fulfilling role and comes with great blessings when you are in alignment with your destiny. He would also say, "that many are called, but few are chosen. Are you ready to do the work of God?"

## Irosun Meji

---

"I stand Tall because of the Ancestors Shoulders I stand Upon."

---

How I became a Sacred Spiritual Light Leader is interesting. I never thought I would be in this role. As I grew up and experienced the many roads of life, it never crossed my mind that my true life's Destiny would be doing spiritual work to help people and make the world a better place to live. When I got into this role, I have always wondered how I got to this point. I had great examples of people in my family always giving back or being committed to improving their community. My father's parents were very active in the Black community. My grandfather would bring strangers home, but my grandmother never questioned it; she just fed the strangers because she knew my grandfather's heart. He was about helping people. My grandfather started the first African American painting company in Cleveland, Ohio, and always gave back to the Black community. My grandmother was giving back to the Black community equally like my grandfather. She co-founded the first African American youth baseball league, G.Y.A.A. (Glenville Youth Athletic Association). I watched her tirelessly giving back to the community, creating fundraisers for the baseball league, and being very committed to her church activities.

My father was the posterboard for hard work, taking care of his immediate and extended family. He gave so much and never wanted anything back. When people called my father for help, he was consistently there and never let anyone down. My father would talk with me about how much time he spent with his grandfather in Chicago. My great-grandfather was a Methodist Minister. In my conversations with my father, he said his grandfather positively affected him in how he treated people and gave back to the world. My father thought he would be a minister because of his time with his grandfather. Even though my father never became a minister or held any titles, he carried the energy and work ethic innately like a Sacred Spiritual Light Leader.

When I started studying my family history on my father's side of the family, the maternal side, I came across some treasured information that made me realize why I am so attracted to Spirituality, metaphysics, and mysticism. The glimpses of my magnetism to these entities started when I was 16 years old in high school. I stopped going to church and started a divine expedition that has been nonstop for 40 years. The prized information I came across about my Ancestors on my father's side of the family was that all my paternal Grandfathers were ministers, primarily Methodist ministers. This information was also revealed to me when I was Initiated in 2019 Into the West African Spiritual system of Ifa. During my Initiation, it was shown through the Sacred Odu (spiritual scripture) Ofun Irosun that my Spiritual affinity is connected to my Ancestors on my father's side and that I come from an infinite line of Spiritual fathers that goes back beyond seven generations: this planet, Universe, as well as time and space. This role was ordained for me by the Universe; it is in my D.N.A.

My ancestors traveled the religious path to do this spiritual work. I am doing the same work today through the spiritual, metaphysical, and mystical paths. In 1997, I met one of my spiritual teachers and Big Brother Baba Ifatumbi Imani Bakari; he was instrumental in helping me understand Spirituality. I thought religion and Spirituality were the same, not realizing that they are different roads. Spirituality is the parent, and religion is the child. At that time, Baba Bakari and I started a men's support group to allow men to share ideas and best practices for navigating life. We would gather once a month and have a circle of dialogue on these best practices. It was a defining auspicious moment that propelled me into the early beginnings of becoming a Sacred Spiritual Light Leader. The meetings were very positive, but we got to the point where the group had to be challenged. The divine message came through Baba Bakari; he said, "Brothers, it's good we are getting together, but the Universe is asking that as a group, we start to practice Spirituality." The room got quiet, faces looked perplexed, and 90 % of the men left the group after that meeting.

I realized at this moment that I did not know the difference between Spirituality and religion, and it was an awakening moment for what was to come for me as a Sacred Spiritual Lightworker. After this awakening moment, my work as a Sacred Spiritual Light Leader took off at warp speed. I found myself going into the prisons helping men transition into everyday life with self-help concepts; this program was called Traveling Back to the Crossroads to Freedom. I worked with young men ages 18 to 30 on manhood and rites of passage. In 2000, I met my godparents/spiritual teachers, Iya Osunnike and Baba Koleoso. They opened the door and saw in me what I couldn't see; the light of Obatala, the love of Oshun, and the Awo mysticism of Orunmila in me. Iya Osunnike, My Godmother, said, "Baba saw your dedication and commitment to the path regardless of your shortcomings." Iya and Baba saw my potential and entrusted me with certain spiritual leadership positions within the Institute because of what they saw in me. I am very grateful for them allowing me to shine in the roles they have bequeathed upon me. I am also thankful to Baba Bakari for taking me under his wing as a little brother who knew nothing about spirituality but also gave me specific spiritual tasks within the Nashville Brotherhood circle. Because of these opportunities that Iya Osunnike, Baba Koleoso, and Baba Bakari placed on me, I am now living in my truth and following my destiny without confusion. Most importantly, it has put me consciously on the path of Sacred Spiritual Light Leadership.

My father, Marshall Henderson Sr., and I were conversing one day about my birth; he said, "When you were born, your mother and I knew you were special; the family knew as well." I did not take that egotistically. That conversation made me think about my destiny; why was I incarnated on this plane of life at this time? What is my purpose on this planet earth? When my father and I had this conversation, I had practiced spirituality for at least 17 years. This conversation with my father made me realize that my gifts and path of spirituality were illuminated like the sun, and many people saw it in me. This was another significant moment on my life journey and spiritual path. I could hear the Universe speaking are you ready to be serious about your Sacred Spiritual Light Leadership mission and again, I could hear Baba Koleoso say, "Are you ready to do God's work?"

## Oyeku Ogbe

---

"I have come to this earth to fulfill my destined mission. I tread only along the path carved out for me by almighty God".

---

I have incarnated in this lifetime as a Sacred Spiritual Light Leader. My mission is to help make the world a better place to live in. The mission to make the world a better place is layered with many tasks and challenges and does not have one specific issue to take on. I will accomplish these universal undertakings using the inborn tools the universe has blessed me with. The spiritual work I have been assigned varies and will always challenge me to be ready no matter the circumstances. My spiritual work is extensive;

"It cannot be put into a box." My spiritual work falls under three main components, which my God Parents, Baba Koleoso and Iya Osunnike, created for the Institute of Whole Life Healing: Know Thy Self, Cleanse and Purify, and Living in Alignment with Absolute Truth. These three spiritual concepts will lead a being/soul toward spiritual liberation: the goal for souls/beings incarnating into this plane of life. Through these three concepts, I specialize in many spiritual practices that help lead beings to spiritual liberation. Divination/readings help people create and understand their life's blueprint, walk in their truth, and understand their blessings and blockages. Spiritual counseling is to give wise counsel and be a strong support for those looking for answers about their spiritual path. Spiritual cleansing helps remove negative energies and attachments accumulated from birth and previous lives. Spiritual initiation helps those initiates walk down the path of truth to meet the universal teacher: the ultimate teacher in life. Spiritual initiation in the mystical realm of life (Death) helps those beings leave their body and elevate them into their next phase of life. A couple of other practices are Reiki, which is an energetic form of healing using the sacred symbols and illuminating colors of the universe to help beings heal and ignite. Also, the Universal Lodge, known as the Sweat Lodge, cleanses and purifies those who need grounding and cleansing and want to astral travel.

Additionally, I strive to assist in healing traumas, including generational, ancestor, and past-life spells, as well as to cleanse and purify. Remember, there are many paths to one truth.

## Conclusion

Our planet needs much help; you never know what mission you are being called on as a Sacred Spiritual Light Leader. The quest is never in a routine fashion; you must always be ready for the unexpected. There is never a dull moment with the many roles I hold: Chief, Senior Priest, Reiki Master, Metaphysical Minister, Babalawo (Orunmila Priest), Babalosha (Priest of Oshun), Egun Priest (working with death and the ancestors), Sweat Lodge Leader, Fire Keeper, and Spiritual Coach. You do not get to pick what work you will do as a Sacred Spiritual Light Leader. The Universe will send those to you based on your elevation and expansion. Direct experience is a prerequisite.

I must admit I have had challenges accepting the role of Sacred Spiritual Light Leadership. Much of it was due to my insecurities and not understanding the position. I often fought with myself about not wanting to be in this role. My life was out of balance because I have battled this many times. I was beginning to learn that because I was not living in my truth, the jobs I worked in corporate America as a supervisor and manager were not ready for my light and truth. I struggled for many years, thinking that I would move up the corporate ladder because I had an MBA. Little did I know that my real job in this lifetime was to be a Sacred Spiritual Light Leader.

Baba Koleoso insisted on how he was supposed to be a lawyer; he had graduated from Ohio University with a J.D. (Juris Doctorate) in Law. Baba Koleoso said the Universe had different plans for him, to serve the people and make the world a better place. Baba didn't practice Law, but he practiced spiritual Law. He served the Universe with many paths and one truth, and the body of his spiritual work encompassed a diverse road of many spiritual systems that empowered him to be a King, Chief, and high priest with quality work. Baba's story always reminds me why living in alignment with your truth is so important.

I am now just getting comfortable with this title because I realize it is part of my truth, my destiny, and one of the main reasons why I incarnated in this lifetime. I know I have a lot of work to do before I transition off this plane of life. Yes, I am ready and maturing more and more every day spiritually. I am very grateful to be able to make the world better than when I came into it. I will continue to be a student of the Universe and let the Universe teach and guide me on all levels. Thank you to the infinite divine energy known as creation, the forces of nature, the divine feminine, the divine masculine, and my ancestors. Thank you to my Mother and Father, my spiritual teachers, and those I have helped and will continue to help in this lifetime. I am grateful to be a Sacred Spiritual Light Leader.

# Chief Awo Falegunwa Osunwole Omitosin Marshall Henderson Jr.

Chief Awo Falegunwa Osunwole Omitosin (Marshall Henderson Jr), is the Senior Priest within the Institute of Whole Life Healing. Baba is also an ardent student of the universe, Mystic, ordained Metaphysical minister, Priest of Orunmila (Babalawo), Priest of Oshun and Egun in the Ifa tradition. Over the past 20 years he has also been initiated as a Fire Keeper and sweat lodge Leader in the Native American tradition, Reiki Master, spiritual healer, and Life coach.

Those who know Baba, know that his mission is to help people live in alignment with their sacred destiny by recognizing the gifts and tools that they have become imbued with through the Universe. Most importantly, he guides those who are called along the path to becoming spiritually liberated, and highly elevated souls before making their transition from earth to the mystical realms of life (Heaven). Join him on this quest.

# Harness the Wisdom of the Orisha for Organizational Success

## Cynthia Oya Gbemi Barnes, Esq.

Step into a world where ancient wisdom converges with contemporary leadership in the workplace. Drawing inspiration from my own experiences, including my Priesthood initiation guided by the co-founders of the Institute of Whole Life Healing, the concept of superior leadership began revealing itself to me.

In this exploration of workplace dynamics, I unveil the impact leadership has on the energy that flows within organizations. Drawing from the wisdom of the Orisha, the revered elemental deities of Yoruba culture, I unravel the secrets of superior leadership that have remained hidden in plain sight. Each Orisha brings a unique essence that, when balanced, fosters a harmonious and productive work environment where both individuals and organizations can thrive.

Through stories, this chapter explores how the elemental energies of Eshu, Oya, Shango, and Oshun, have shown up during my journey. These narratives offer fresh insights into the energy imbalances that can hinder personal growth and organizational success. My intention for you as you read this chapter is that you'll emerge with the wisdom of a Priestess, ready to navigate workplace complexities with insight, grace, and ease.

Are you ready to balance the energy within yourself or your workplace? Explore further possibilities and seize leadership coaching opportunities by contacting Priestess Oya Gbemi at:

www.disruptorganization.com

# From Crisis to Integration –
## Weaving Spiritual and Professional Paths

The philosophy of the Institute of Whole Life Healing (IWLH) is that it seeks no followers. However, after eighteen years, I am still committed, growing, and learning with the IWLH. The wholistically designed Mind/Body Soul/Spirit (MBS) blueprint is the foundation of its initiations. The MBS blueprint is based on three universal principles: (1) Know Thyself; (2) Cleanse and Purify; and (3) Live in Alignment with Absolute Truth.

*I recall my first interactions with Iya and Baba. As I found myself in yet another spiritual crisis, compounded by professional challenges at work that included discrimination and being repeatedly overlooked for promotions despite my qualifications, I was seeking guidance. I was searching for Grisso, who was the preeminent teacher for the Metu Neter: The Great Oracle of the Tehuti and the Egyptian System of Spiritual Cultivation. I tried reaching Grisso using several phone numbers that I had found on the internet. When I called the fifth number, Iya answers. She tells me that Grisso was displaced by hurricane Katrina and the last she heard he was in Atlanta. She did not have his current contact information. I had an emotional breakdown on the call. I really need someone to teach me the Metu Neter oracle system. Iya tells me that she and her husband, Baba, could give me a whole life reading and perhaps that could give me some direction. Although I couldn't recall anything specifically about the Whole Life Reading without referring to my notes, I remember how comfortable I felt with Iya and Baba. I also remember at the end, Iya saying she would like to send me an introductory letter for the Sacred Feminine Mysteries (SFM) initiation and if I was interested to let her know.*

Less than 90 days after this Divinely guided call connected me to the IWLH, I started my Sacred Feminine Mysteries (SFM) initiation, which lasted eighteen months. The SFM initiation is structured around the MBS blueprint. Each universal principle was a step in the SFM process, which had four different lessons that included readings from various religious and spiritual traditions as well as assignments. During Step 1, Know Thyself, I learned tools to uncover my beliefs and coping mechanisms, to explore the energy body, and to understand the law of attraction. During Step 2, Cleanse and Purify, I learned tools to transform outdated beliefs and coping mechanisms, to re-balance the energy body, and to change how things were attracted into my life. During Step 3, Live in Alignment with Absolute Truth, I learned to recognize from my emotional state and my energy level when I am not in integrity with my Truth. Almost ten years after my SFM initiation, I started the Journey to Priesthood (JTP) initiation with the IWLH. Using the same MBS blueprint, I started an in-depth study of Orisha, revered deities in the Yoruba culture and began to get a glimpse of superior leadership. Superior leadership is the art of fostering individual growth that inspires and guides the individual to achieve both personal and collective goals simultaneously for the highest and best good of all involved.

## Sacred Spirit Light Worker: Workplace Energy Dynamics

The realm of workplace energy dynamics embodies the unseen forces that shape the atmosphere and interactions within an organization. Workplace energy dynamics are the result of the flow, exchange, and influence of energies among individuals, teams, and leaders in the work environment. This concept extends beyond the tangible metrics of productivity and performance, delving into the subtleties of relationships, communication, and the emotional resonance that underpins organizational functioning. Understanding the significance of workplace energy dynamics is vital as it profoundly impacts employee well-being, collaboration, communication, and the ability to constructively address challenges. Ultimately, the workplace environment's overall vibrancy, coherence, and success depend on balancing the energy within and among individuals, teams, and leaders.

Within the workplace context, the Orisha, revered deities in the Yoruba culture, offer profound insights and practical applications for shaping organizational culture, communication, leadership, and problem-solving. Each Orisha brings a unique essence that, when balanced, fosters a harmonious and productive work environment. Recognizing and understanding the imbalances in these energies is crucial for navigating the complexities of workplace dynamics. Embracing the wisdom of the Orishas provides a framework to promote balance, innovation, and collaborative synergy, creating an environment where both individuals and organizations can thrive. This exploration of the Orisha in workplace energy dynamics aims to shed light on how Eshu, Oya, Shango, and Oshun have shown up in my experiences.

## Eshu: Facilitating Adaptability and Decision-Making

Eshu, the Orisha representing crossroads, communication, and adaptability, brings a unique influence to workplace energy dynamics. His essence embodies the essence of adaptability, effective communication, and the critical role of decision-making in organizational settings.

In an imbalanced form, Eshu's essence in workplace energy results in chaotic communication and an unpredictable environment. This imbalance leads to a lack of clarity, misinterpretation of information, and a disorganized flow of ideas. There may be an overemphasis on constant change without a clear direction, causing confusion and frustration among team members. The lack of stability and consistency due to excessive adaptability leads to an environment where decisions are made impulsively, hindering the creation of structured plans, and fostering an atmosphere of unpredictability. The imbalanced energy of Eshu impedes productivity and the establishment of cohesive strategies. Communication breakdowns and disarray from unbalanced Eshu energy create an environment of uncertainty and unrest among employees.

*I ventured off into a trucking business for about three years without a contract with someone I considered a brother and a friend. We started a trucking company using my cash and credit to purchase a refrigerated truck. I read the Department of Transportation (DOT) regulations, set the business up, and passed the DOT inspection with ease. He used his contacts to secure loads and generate revenue. He was a good and safe driver. He kept revenue coming in; however, he was not consistent with his DOT paperwork, and we failed to discuss how to manage the cash flow in the business. About two and half years into the trucking business, his wife showed up with a brand-new Cadillac and I realized that when he was taking out cash advances it was more than what was needed to pay for fuel: the imbalanced energy of Eshu. I was under the impression that we were both working towards a goal of getting the truck paid off so we both could enjoy a positive cash flow. However, in the end, I would be out of my initial investment and have the tax liability for the company solely on my shoulders.*

In the workplace, Eshu's energy symbolizes adaptability and flexibility. He encourages individuals and organizations to navigate complex situations and change with agility. Embracing Eshu's energy involves fostering a work environment where individuals readily adapt to shifting circumstances, allowing for quick thinking and a willingness to embrace new perspectives and solutions. Eshu's influence underscores the importance of effective communication. Encouraging clear and open communication channels within the workplace, where ideas and information flow freely, is integral to channeling Eshu's energy. A transparent and inclusive communication culture fosters understanding and allows for better collaboration and problem-solving.

*My imbalanced Eshu experience was a great lesson to ensure that there is clear communication before launching into a new business venture. Now, I enter into business ventures clearly understanding the cash flow and expectations of all parties. As the COVID pandemic unfolded, I found myself being laid off along with millions of others around the world. During the week before I was laid off, I was spending my mornings volunteering at the food bank making lunches for school-age children. At lunchtime, I was on an inspirational call that was being led by a serial entrepreneur and CEO woman, showing us how to create a business plan. If you drafted a business plan, you could pitch it to the CEO at the end of the week and she would provide you with feedback. As I was nearing the end of my business plan proposal to the CEO, she stopped me and told me that she needed me on her team. By the middle of the next week, we had ironed out the details in a contract. Over the next eighteen months, I would have the opportunity to travel to both Turkey and Thailand using my legal, engineering, and process improvement skills.*

Practical applications of Eshu's influence in the workplace involve promoting adaptability and enhancing communication. By embodying Eshu's adaptable energy, organizations can navigate change and challenges with greater ease, fostering an environment where quick thinking, open communication, and flexible decision-making are encouraged. This approach promotes a more resilient and agile organizational culture and allows for greater innovation and problem-solving capabilities.

# Oya: Catalyst for Transformation and Change

Oya, the Orisha embodying transformation and change, holds a crucial position in shaping workplace energy dynamics be it reorganization, shifts in leadership, or alterations in company direction. Her essence permeates the environment during periods of conflict and change offering insights that can significantly impact organizational culture and employee interactions. Her message resonates in the need for adaptability and the courage to confront uncertainties.

In the workplace, an imbalanced essence of Oya manifests as resistance to change and an aversion to addressing conflicts or transitions. This imbalance results in an environment where fear of change prevails, hindering progress and growth. Individuals may exhibit a defensive stance, leading to a lack of adaptability and an unwillingness to explore new ideas or approaches. The energy of Oya, when imbalanced, fosters an atmosphere where unresolved conflicts linger, stifling open communication and impeding the resolution of issues. This imbalance creates a stagnant and tense workplace, hindering the organization's ability to evolve and thrive in an ever-changing landscape.

*The imbalanced energy of Oya is demonstrated in a work experience in my early twenties. I worked at the McDonalds on Twelfth Street in Erie, Pennsylvania. During that time the food was made in batches and set in cues ready for customers to order. Like most fast-food places during that time the place was always busy with activity. Orders coming in from the drive-thru and from customers waiting inside in line. Employees were required to wear a standard uniform that consisted of the McDonald's yellow and red hat and shirt, black pants, and nonslip shoes. We were like robots working behind the counters following the directives of whatever manager was on duty. I wasn't a leader at this time, just a cashier. I was a hard worker. I showed up on time and mostly followed the orders that were barked at me. Eventually, my leadership potential was recognized by the store manager, who offered me a managerial position that I declined since it required me to drop out of college. After I declined the manager position, I noticed my work assignments started changing. My consistent hours became sporadic. Then, one day I arrived at work to find my work assignment was cleaning the bathroom. You must be kidding me I am not cleaning a public bathroom! The Oya in me was reluctant to face the changes that were happening, so I moved onto other opportunities.*

In the workplace, Oya's energy reflects the winds of change. She beckons individuals and organizations to embrace transitions as opportunities for growth rather than as intimidating disruptions. Embracing Oya's influence means acknowledging the inevitability of change and fostering a mindset that adapts swiftly to new circumstances, welcoming innovation, and new perspectives. She teaches us that conflicts, though daunting, hold the key to growth and transformation. Her essence offers lessons on managing disputes and tensions with grace and resilience. Rather than avoiding conflicts, she teaches the significance of engaging with them constructively. Oya's energy invites open communication, active listening, and an understanding that conflicts, when addressed with integrity and empathy (an open heart), can lead to breakthroughs and stronger relationships.

*Early in 2008, I had the opportunity to attend a workshop with Colin Tipping, who was the author of the Radical Forgiveness book, and his wife, JoAnna. He was holding a radical forgiveness workshop at a retreat center in Dahlonega, Georgia. I had read the book and did many radical forgiveness worksheets over the previous six months. I went to the retreat expecting to do the same. On the first night, we were introduced to Satori, the Radical Forgiveness game that Colin and his wife created. My first thought was I paid to play a game? Now, I have to have a talk with myself, so I don't check out and miss what I am supposed to learn here. After the retreat I purchased the Radical Forgiveness game for myself because the game helped me learn how to tell the story differently. Whenever I have an issue that comes up and I feel I need some clarity around it, I'd play the game. You start the game by picking two cards: an event card and a context card. Thinking about the context and the event card, you tell a story from the victim's perspective. The game is a spiral that starts outside in victim land and spirals inside through three gateways until you reach the center, Satori. The outside spiral is victim land where your beliefs create a web that blocks energy flow, where you project your unconscious belief onto others, where you blame others for your situation, and Karma just runs the show. Then you reach the first gateway of awareness where you are willing to be open to the possibility that the experience is happening to for you not to you, you begin to practice self-acceptance, and you learn to use your breath to release energy blocks in your body. Now in this gateway, you might get delayed in your healing process, called a spiritual bypass, because you are really just going through the motions. Eventually, you get to the second gateway where the shift happens. In this gateway, you continue to use your healing breath to release energy blocks, you pick up new stories, and you recognize that those people involved in your conflict are really healing angels for you and you are healing angels for them. Now you approach the third gateway of surrender where you finish releasing all that has held you back, recognize your oneness with all things, and surrender to the possibility that everything happens for a reason.*

*Fast forward to the fall of 2008, amid the Great Recession when manufacturing companies were downsizing. My employer had an all-employees meeting to advise us that they were going to be downsizing over the next few months. My intuition was telling me that I was going to be impacted by this downsizing. Over the next few months, I leaned into the change that Oya was bringing into my life as I played the Radical Forgiveness game regularly to deal with the emotions that were coming up as I slowly took personal items out of my office. In the spring of 2009, my supervisor and human resources called me into an office and advised me that I was being laid off. Security would escort me from the meeting to my office to gather my belongings, which at this point fit into one banker's box, and then to my car.*

Practical applications of Oya's influence involve fostering a workplace culture that values adaptability, resilience, and open dialogue. Embracing change as an opportunity for growth, encouraging diverse perspectives, and navigating conflicts with understanding and empathy are integral to integrating Oya's essence into the workplace. By embodying Oya's transformative energy, organizations can create an environment that embraces change and harnesses it for collective advancement and innovation, fostering a culture of adaptability, resilience, and strength.

## Shango: Leadership, Strength, and Power

Shango, the Orisha symbolizing leadership, strength, and power, embodies qualities crucial to workplace dynamics. His energy reverberates in the realm of effective leadership, where strength meets wisdom, and power aligns with responsibility. In the workplace, harnessing Shango's essence can transform the very fabric of organizational structures and employee interactions.

In an imbalanced state, Shango's essence in workplace energy may manifest as an authoritarian and overpowering leadership style. This imbalance could lead to a workplace environment dominated by an excessive focus on power and control, hindering open collaboration and stifling the growth of innovative ideas. The imbalanced Shango energy may foster an atmosphere where leadership becomes more about asserting authority than empowering and guiding team members. This imbalance might result in a lack of inclusivity, as the pursuit of power may overshadow the need for fostering a supportive and empowering environment. The overwhelming focus on dominance and authority could lead to an environment where individual growth and the exploration of diverse viewpoints take a back seat, hindering the potential for a truly collaborative and dynamic workplace.

*As I look back at the times when the winds of Oya brought change into my life, I notice that the leadership during those times tended to exhibit an imbalanced Shango energy. After evaluating the pros and cons of taking a promotion or finishing the bachelor's degree in engineering, I turned down a promotion. In response, my manager asserted his authority by reducing my hours and assigning me to clean the bathrooms. In another experience later in my career, my manager before the layoff during the Great Recession, had started with the company the prior year as the Purchasing Director. She came in and immediately started making changes to procedures and processes based on her prior work experience without any input from her staff. Although she survived the layoff in 2009, her imbalanced leadership style would cause the company to let her go the following year.*

At the heart of Shango's influence lies the essence of leadership. Shango encourages a leadership style that blends strength and resilience with empathy and understanding. Leaders embodying Shango's energy inspire through their robustness and remain receptive to their team's needs and concerns. They exemplify strength not in dominance but in fostering an environment where every voice is heard and valued. Moreover, Shango's energy reveals the delicate balance between power and responsibility. In the workplace, this balance is vital to cultivate a healthy, equitable environment. It is not merely about wielding authority but about utilizing power in service of collective goals, maintaining accountability, and ensuring fair decision-making processes.

*My first internship with a Fortune 500 company while pursuing my bachelor's degree in mechanical engineering was in the purchasing department. My supervisor at that time gave me the most valuable lesson that continues to influence my leadership style today. During the first week of work and before getting too immersed in the day-to-day responsibilities of ordering motor hardware, my supervisor took me downstairs to the shop floor where the motors were manufactured and assembled. I was fascinated with the flow and the rhythm created by the sound of the machines moving parts and the mechanics assembling various parts that go into a motor. Then suddenly, my supervisor grabbed my ear and pulled me closer to him so I could hear his words over the machine sounds. He says, "Whenever you are going to make any change to a part be sure to come down to the shop floor and discuss it with the mechanics that use the part."*

*Just a few years later, I would find myself in a small rural town in Illinois for a six-month assignment managing an area of the manufacturing floor. The employees were hostile to me simply because of my youth. I recall being told that I was just like all the other young college graduates who came through who didn't know anything about the process and then got a promotion to another business. I could see their perspective. It was already hard enough for me to be an African-American woman engineer. Their feelings towards me made me feel isolated. Remembering my first corporate manager's lesson, I decided to take time to learn each person's job and find out what issues they faced. It was in this job that I developed my philosophy about being a leader. A leader's role is to help remove barriers so that employees can do their job. I know that I left an impact on the people that worked for me during that assignment. As I was graduating from the management training program and accepted a full-time position in Ohio, my employees had a going away party for me where they gave me a card and where each person signed their name and taped a folded bill.*

Practically applying Shango's influence involves nurturing leadership that upholds ethical conduct, integrity, and transparency. It involves empowering employees to take charge of their roles, fostering an environment where strengths are celebrated, and individuals are encouraged to grow within their positions. Understanding Shango's essence in the workplace is recognizing the significance of responsible and empathetic leadership, empowering individuals while fostering a culture where power is wielded judiciously for the collective advancement of the organization. Integrating Shango's qualities can significantly enhance workplace dynamics, instilling a sense of purpose, balance, and strength within the organizational framework.

## Oshun: Nurturing Harmony and Creativity

Oshun, the Orisha symbolizing harmony, creativity, and abundance, offers profound insights that greatly influence workplace energy dynamics. Her essence resonates in the environment, fostering an atmosphere where collaboration, creativity, and positive relationships thrive.

In an imbalanced form, Oshun's essence in workplace energy reflects an overindulgence in harmony at the cost of productivity. This imbalance might lead to an overly lax environment, where the pursuit of creative ideas and collaboration becomes secondary to maintaining a comfortable and conflict-free atmosphere. This excessive focus on positivity and harmony could deter necessary conflict resolution, hindering growth and progress. Imbalanced Oshun energy might lead to a workplace where individuals prioritize consensus over constructive critique, leading to a lack of diverse perspectives and potentially hindering innovation. This excessive pursuit of harmony might overlook necessary challenges or necessary adjustments, resulting in an environment where essential issues are left unaddressed, impeding growth and development within the organization.

*I was working in a union plant where I had responsibility for 24-hour production. My shift supervisors were also members of the union. I did not want to put my supervisors in a controversial position with other union members. Therefore, I developed a routine of showing up at random times during the second and third shifts to meet employees, to learn about the challenges employees faced, and to check on the operations. I had heard rumors from other employees about employees sleeping during work hours; however, the employees were not willing to come forward publicly. One day I showed up around 2 a.m. and found several women sleeping in the restroom. Based on my own observations, I wrote the women up and placed the disciplinary record in their employee file. This happened in the year before the contract negotiations between the company and the union. The union president threatened a strike if I proceeded with disciplining the employees and began attacking my managerial skills. It crushed my confidence when the plant manager and the human resources manager made me withdraw the discipline from the employees file. Over the next few months, I slipped into a pit of despair. I am so angry that I feel my insides burning up every day I go to work. I felt abandoned by business leaders around the company, who were advising me to look for another job. Why am I looking for another job I ask? Well, I'm told that if contract negotiations failed the following year, I would be the scapegoat. I leveraged the discord to secure a promotion. The union ratified the contract that year. However, over the next ten years, the plant's productivity would continue to decline, and the plant was eventually closed.*

In the workplace, Oshun's energy reflects the essence of harmonious collaboration. Her influence encourages a culture that values positive relationships, empathy, and the celebration of diversity. Nurturing Oshun's energy means creating a space where individuals feel valued, respected, and encouraged to express their unique perspectives, contributing to a collective symphony of ideas. Moreover, Oshun's presence ignites the spark of creativity within the workplace. Her essence inspires innovative thinking, artistic expression, and the exploration of new solutions. Embracing Oshun's energy involves encouraging a culture that values and nurtures creativity, offering space for experimentation and honoring diverse approaches to problem-solving.

*My experience learning the Six Sigma process for my project and mentoring Green Belt projects was the epitome of Oshun's balanced energy manifesting in the workplace. I was leading projects in manufacturing facilities where the machine mechanics had been working on their equipment for more years than I had been alive. During my first year learning the Six Sigma process with my own project, I mentored thirteen Green Belt projects that were all successful even though I knew nothing about the specific manufacturing process. During my second year, I had one project, and the mechanic was convinced that the rejection rate on his equipment could not be improved without purchasing new equipment. Instead of pushing the mechanic, I organized an opportunity for him to take his first-ever road trip to another facility that had similar equipment to his so that he could collaborate with mechanics whose equipment had fewer rejections. Upon return to his facility, the mechanic was inspired to support me in reducing the rejection rate on his equipment.*

Practical applications of Oshun's influence involve fostering an inclusive workplace culture that celebrates diversity, empathy, and creativity. By fostering an environment where everyone's voice is heard, and individuals feel encouraged to express their creativity, organizations can harness Oshun's essence to foster an environment that thrives on innovation, collaboration, and a collective pursuit of excellence. Embodying Oshun's harmonious energy in the workplace creates a space where positivity, creativity, and inclusivity flourish, contributing to a vibrant and thriving organizational culture.

# Conclusion

In the vibrant tapestry of workplace energy dynamics, the influences of Eshu, Oya, Shango, and Oshun interweave to shape a multifaceted organizational environment. Eshu's adaptable essence calls for flexibility in communication and decision-making, fostering an agile workplace that navigates change with ease. Oya's transformative energy encourages embracing change and resolving conflicts, paving the way for growth and adaptability within the organization. Shango's leadership qualities advocate for responsible and empowering guidance, promoting strength while nurturing a collaborative environment. Oshun's harmonious essence underscores the importance of creativity and positive relationships, cultivating an environment that thrives on innovation and inclusivity. By recognizing and balancing these energies, workplaces can create a harmonious ecosystem that celebrates adaptability, transformative growth, responsible leadership, and a culture that fosters both creativity and harmonious collaboration among individuals.

Iya's offer to introduce me to the Sacred Feminine Mysteries (SFM) initiation marked the beginning of a profound spiritual journey and planted the seeds for a unique integration of my priestess path with my professional life.

# Priestess Oya Gbemi

Cynthia "Oya Gbemi" Barnes, a mechanical engineer, attorney, reference librarian, and professor, currently serves as the Institute's board chairperson. She embodies the Institute's philosophy of Many Paths One Truth. As a Priestess, reiki master, intuitive sound healer, and diviner, Oya Gbemi knows how to live in the center of the hurricane of life experiences. She has a deep passion for helping you transform the experiences that manifest in your life.

Oya Gbemi's strength lies in her ability to guide you on the journey beyond the mysterious realm of emotions to the sacred within to recognize unconscious core beliefs and outdated coping mechanisms that are running your life like a scratched record repeating. She then supports you to use the sword of truth to transform beliefs that no longer serve your highest and greatest good allowing you to emerge with the power and energy to rule your life.

# A Cosmic Love Story
## Lisa AyoDeji Allen & Ralph L. Stevenson

When my first-born daughter invited me to co-author a writing project with her, I was delighted to have an opportunity to take a stroll down memory lane reflecting on our special journey together. In the spirit of gratitude and appreciation, I give thanks to the gift and blessing for this beautiful soul that we have come to know as Lisa "AyoDeji".

It was/is just what the doctor ordered for me at this moment in time and space of my life, to reflect and share memories and information regarding our respective individual and collective life-walk. This cosmic love story is about a father and daughter finding each other after 18 years of separation and their beautiful journey following.

Spiritual, cosmic, and energetic connections traverse lifetimes and cannot be easily severed. Separated almost two decades did not lessen the intensity of our genuine and authentic connection. I encourage you, the reader, to stay true to who you are and follow your passions; through that process you will be connected to others known and unknown who will support you on your journey.

# The Dynamic Duo

This beautiful love story between father and daughter is cosmic and karmic. Reunited, we are two light leaders with a passion for self-discovery and sharing our gifts with the world. As we see it, we all come from the same source, no matter the different names. Many paths. One truth.

As spiritual beings, having a human experience, we all have this amazing opportunity to come together in support of bringing balance back to this world. It's not about separation. It's about wholeness. We are one!

# The Beginning

**Dad:** Our relationship as father and daughter began in a non-traditional family structure because AyoDeji's mother and I were dating and not married at the time of her birth. However, as circumstances would have it, AyoDeji's mother and I went on to marry other people before AyoDeji was a year old, which created dynamics that prevented AyoDeji and me from being a part of each other's lives for 18 years.

As I recall, one of the primary reasons for the 18 years of separation was because of AyoDeji's stepfather, who met AyoDeji's mom not long after she had given birth. He was willing to step up and marry AyoDeji's mom and take full responsibility as AyoDeji's father with the understanding that I would not interfere and complicate matters.

Even though that decision made sense on some level, and I agreed, especially considering that I also married someone else, I always felt a strong psychic/spiritual pull to see her and be a part of her life. I did not push back because of the dynamics that shaped the situation.

As a result of this strong pull and/or perhaps curiosity, from time to time over those 18 years, I would drive down the block where she lived, sometimes parking, and hoping to catch a glimpse of someone who might be my daughter.

During AyoDeji's entire childhood, she remained under the impression that her stepfather was her biological father. As fate would have it, 18 years later, I happened to board the same bus that AyoDeji's mom was on and when I inquired about connecting with AyoDeji, she informed me that she and her husband were no longer together and was happy to schedule a time for me to come to her house to meet my daughter.

When that day arrived, I was experiencing some anxiety, a sense of awkwardness and excitement all at the same time. I knocked on the door, AyoDeji opened the door, and when our eyes connected, I experienced a rush of emotions knowing intuitively that this beautiful soul was truly my daughter.

Prior to this day, the only times I saw AyoDeji was when I traveled to Brooklyn, New York, where she was born and visited both AyoDeji and her mom who were living with AyoDeji's great uncle.

I would like to share with you how that first contact went from AyoDeji's perspective because she wrote about the experience and included it in her first Happy Father's Day card to me:

*The year was 1982 and graduating from high school was a big event for my family. Being the eldest of five children, I had to set the example. I was all set to attend Lincoln University, the oldest Black university in the country and part of the Underground Railroad. I was excited and proud to be finally getting the chance to get away from the crazy streets of Philly.*

*A few months before leaving for school, my mother decided to have a Pokeno party. Everybody I knew was down for that. Eating fried chicken, gambling and talkin' much trash was a great way to pass the time on a hot Saturday afternoon.*

*The house was full of folks when there was a knock at the door. I answered (opened) the door to a man who looked to be in his early forties and dressed kinda casual with a cheerful smile. He asked if my mom was home. I invited him in and yelled upstairs to my mom letting her know she had company waiting. The gentleman was no* one I could ever remember seeing before. Mom had many friends, but his face was unfamiliar to me. The strange thing was that he smiled at me each time I looked his way. I began to wonder, who is this old pervert?

Since mom was taking a lifetime to come downstairs and attend to her company, I asked the gentleman if he knew how to play Pokeno. He admitted that he did not. I escorted him to a table of full screaming, crazy folks fighting over cards. I let him pick out a Pokeno card and proceeded to explain the ins and outs of the game. Finally, mom decided to make her grand entrance. They walked into the living room and began to talk. He stayed a little while longer and then said his farewell. By the end of the day, I won $5.56 in pennies and had my fill of chicken, potato chips and kool-aid. I was exhausted and slept like a rock.

The next morning, I got up early and went downstairs for my daily bowl of Cap'n Crunch. My mom was busy doing the dishes. I grabbed my bowl and hustled the milk out of the refrigerator. As I am filling my bowl to capacity with those hard, crunchy bits of heaven, my mom asked, "Do you remember the man who came to see me yesterday?" I replied, "Sure." She then asked, "Do you think you look like him?" I answered, "No, should I?" During this conversation, it never once occurred to me what she was trying to tell me. For the past 18 years, I was led to believe that the man who brought home the paychecks occasionally, who took us to the drive-in movies, and who went ballistic after a 5th of vodka was my father. I had no reason to believe otherwise, until today. Mom then replied, a little unsure of herself, "Well, he's your father..." That statement hit me like a lightning bolt. Anything that she said after that, I did not hear. Immediately, questions started flying from my mouth. It seemed as if I had no control. "Where did you meet?" "What happened?" "Why wasn't I told?" "Does dad know?" Mom tried to answer my questions as quickly and honestly as she could.

Once the smoke cleared from the barrage of questions I shot out like an automatic weapon, I found myself going through many mixed emotions. I felt hurt, surprised, happy, suspicious, and curious. Then, I wanted to know more about this mysterious man. Mom had given me his telephone number and told me to call when I felt I was ready. I wasted no time. I dialed the number and waited *anxiously for the voice on the other end. The rest is history...*

*You have been my big brother, my confidant, my guide, my mentor, my guru, and my best friend. I am so very proud to have you in my life. I love you. Happy Father's Day!*

# Walking In Rhythm

**Dad**: We discovered we were old souls who genuinely enjoyed each other's company and enjoyed talking about all kinds of things. During her college days, she shared with me concerns about "out of body experiences (OBEs)" she was having, which prompted me to share with her the OBEs I had mostly in my youth and young adulthood.

I shared with her how frightening the experience was for me and how frustrating it was not to find anyone who could explain to me what I was experiencing other than a couple of elders who told me not to worry, and that it was only the "witch's ride" that I was experiencing. As you can imagine that did not help at all, but on the contrary, made matters worse.

That is all I had to go on, until I purchased a book entitled, Out Of Body Experiences by Dr. Robert Monroe that helped me to grasp what was happening and I immediately shared the book with AyoDeji to provide more insight for her.

"In an out-of-body state you are no longer bounded by time-space. You can be in it but not part of it. You---your non-physical self---are comfortable in another energy system. You have a great sense of freedom. Yet you are not totally free. You are like a balloon or a kite on a tether. At the other end of the cord---the invisible cord---is our physical body." Dr. Robert Monroe

## The Astral Realm Realized

**AyoDeji**: I adapted to college life easily. A natural loner, I spent most of my time in my dorm room when I was not in class. It was in the early morning hours, as I lay in bed that I found myself dreaming. This was an unusual dream. I had floated up to the ceiling and I could see my body lying in the bed below. This dream was so real!

Upon awakening, I called my biological father, who I had met for the first time just a month or so earlier and with whom I was building a budding relationship after 18 years of separation. We connected rather quickly following his initial awkward visit. We shared similar interests in ancient Kemet/Nile Valley Civilization, the cosmos, all things mystical and finding one's purpose. He was a great resource and support for me in those areas.

After explaining my dream, without hesitation, he said, "You had an OBE, an out of body experience." After our chat, he sent me a book by Dr. Robert Monroe who had documented his experiences with OBEs over many years. I practiced the techniques shared in the book every free moment available to me. I had big dreams of astral traveling to anywhere my heart desired.

During a rare weekend visit home to Philly, I was excited to try the astral travel techniques. I tip-toed upstairs to my childhood bedroom trying not to bring attention to myself, as I didn't want to be disturbed. As I lay in the bed, with my eyes closed and my breathing focused and steady, I began to feel a tingling all over my body. The tingling became a buzzing that I could hear and feel inside my head all the way down to my toes. This is it! I thought to myself. I was nervous and a bit scared but kept myself together. I pushed through the fear and put the techniques to work. I tried the rollout method and to my surprise, it worked!

As I rolled out of my body, I floated down to the floor from the bed. With my eyes closed, I remember touching my astral hand to the wooden floor and feeling the nails beneath the wooden floorboards. How could this be? I suddenly remembered that I needed to open my astral eyes to see where I was going. It's a strange phenomenon but you simply have to think about opening your eyes and then you can see! Amazing! I floated over to the closed bedroom door to test if I could go through solid objects. As I touched my astral hand to the bedroom door, I was trying to think about going through it. As I consciously focused on that, I could hear someone coming up the stairs, which led straight back to my bedroom. Spooked, the next thing I remember is flying quickly across the room and jumping back into my body. It was wild!

# Kismet

**Dad**: Being able to share this resource with AyoDeji at a pivotal point in her spiritual growth and development assisted and helped to strengthen our relationship and lay the foundation for more breakthrough adventures to come.

We were really connecting the dots. The more we talked and shared, we discovered a number of patterns and synchronicities, as it related to our individual and collective life walk.

During the early 70s, after several years working in corporate America in sales and marketing, I decided to relocate to Atlanta, Georgia where I finally embarked on a career in education. I was one of the first people of African descent to desegregate an elementary school in Roswell, Georgia and a middle school in Sandy, Springs Georgia.

On a similar path, AyoDeji choose to relocate to Georgia in the early 90s. Moreover, she eventually moved to Sandy Springs, Georgia and right around the corner from Sandy Springs Middle School. She also ended up in Roswell, Georgia during her stay there. Talk about synchronicities!

I don't believe I was consciously aware of it at the time, but along with the experience of desegregating two schools in the South, my years of interest in spiritual growth and development would sometimes find its way into the class lesson. A case in point, even though I did not consider myself a light leader at the time, I initiated a project with my elementary school class entitled, Who Am I? The project required each student to bring in a small headshot photo of himself or herself. Each student received a sheet of construction paper and a stencil of a 5-pointed star that they traced and cut out. On the blackboard, I listed each of the twelve zodiac signs from Aries to Pisces with a list of positive and negative attributes under each along with the element associated with each sign, fire, air, water, and earth. The next step was to jazz up their star art creations with a dab of glue and some sprinkles.

As a class, we continued to build on the idea that stars are made up of energy/light/frequency and each and every one of us are stars in this micro and macro universe, which is also made up of energy, helping to answer the question, Who Am I? Perhaps, subconsciously, in my own way, I was seeding and preparing my 6th grade students for the road less traveled...as light leaders...far removed from my official job description as a classroom schoolteacher.

# Kindred

**AyoDeji**: During my 31 years in Georgia, I was discovering who I was. Like my dad, I don't believe I was consciously aware that I was sharing my gifts with others as a light leader. I was providing tarot card readings for those seeking some guidance and light on their paths. In addition to that, I was working with several new age groups and traveling around the country doing spiritual work related to elevating the ancestors and energetically cleansing certain lands where atrocities had occurred. During this time, my dad was there continuing his support on my path.

The beauty and blessing in our connection, although separated for 18 years initially, is that we get each other. We can talk about anything and everything, including lion people in the sky. How wonderful is that?

# Initiation

**Dad**: Another area of synchronicity for AyoDeji and me is we were the first in our respective generation to leave the Greco-Roman, Judeo-Christian, Islamic religious faiths in favor of indigenous spirituality, metaphysics, esoteric sciences, and related subjects which deepened our bond as father and daughter.

Most of my spiritual and philosophic studies are based on ancient Kemet/Nile Valley Civilization science and culture. AyoDeji's primary studies also based on ancient Kemet/Nile Valley Civilization and indigenous culture led her to go through her first initiation with Baba Ifa Karade. As I sat through the crossing over ceremony of AyoDeji's Shango initiation, I was delighted and proud over my first-born child taking her spiritual quest to the next level of Priestess.

**AyoDeji**: In 2003, I was initiated by Baba Ifa Karade into the energy of the African deity Shango. Shango is often associated with the divine masculine. As an Orisha of thunder and lightning, Shango represents the power and strength of male energy, which is why he is often depicted as a warrior, a leader, and a protector. Through divination, a Babalawo, who is a high priest and diviner in the African Yoruba tradition, determines which orisha has claimed your head, and it is the energy of that particular orisha you are initiated into. It does not matter if you are male or female. It's about the energy, vibration, and frequency of the deity.

This initiation set me on a deeper path to self-discovery. Initiation is much more than just ritual and ceremony. Truth be told, it is really the beginning of a never-ending journey of discovering who you truly are at the core - at the soul level.

I was so honored to have my dad there for my crossing over. It really meant a lot to me because he was the only one in my family who really understood why I went through initiation and how sacred that process was for me.

In 2011, my continuing quest for self-knowledge eventually led me to Iya Osunnike and Baba ji Koleoso, the founders of the Institute of Whole Life Healing. During my 13 years with the Institute, to date, I have been initiated as a priestess of the African deity and goddess Oshun, and also as a Sacred Feminine Mysteries priestess. Being an initiate means being of service to humanity and bringing your light and spiritual gifts to help transmute, heal, illuminate, and ascend.

# An Ancestor Returns

**Dad**: Several years after her Shango initiation, AyoDeji was in Philadelphia for the annual Odunde, an African American festival based on Yoruba tradition. This was AyoDeji's first Odunde experience. I attended (almost) every year since its inception in 1975.

During the festival, we were walking with the procession, complete with drummers and stilt walkers, headed to the river to make offerings to the African deity and goddess, Oshun. The procession stopped prior to crossing the bridge, so that the Yoruba priest, known as a Babalawo, could make prayers before we could give our offerings of fruit, flowers and honey to Oshun represented by the Schuylkill River.

As all of this was happening, AyoDeji suddenly fainted, falling backward into my arms. I was able to sit down on the ground while holding her. When she regained consciousness, she was in a trance speaking fluently in an African dialect that made absolutely no sense to me.

While AyoDeji continued to speak this African language, the Babalawo approached to offer his assistance. When he reached out to touch AyoDeji, she recoiled and began speaking more aggressively in the same African language. The Babalawo stepped back in retreat and seemed somewhat afraid. Having second thoughts, he quickly left us. All I could do was hold AyoDeji, comfort her and reassure her that I was there for her, and everything would be all right. Eventually, a Yoruba woman sat down on the ground next to us and held AyoDeji's hand, while maintaining a conversation in the same African dialect. AyoDeji came out of the possession and the procession to give offerings to Oshun continued. Those possessions happened several times when we were together. I learned the spirit coming through AyoDeji identified herself as Oni, who may have been an African ancestor.

**AyoDeji**: The experience at the Odunde Festival was surreal. I vividly remember speaking an African language and recoiling from the Babalawo's attempted touch because his energy did not "feel" genuine. It felt as if Oni knew that this Babalawo was not who he appeared to be on the outside, with all his regalia and entourage. She could feel those dark places within him and sensed an abuse of power against women. It was very intense. This would explain the rage and pain Oni exhibited whenever she came through. It was always through tears, a deep wailing, and a sense of urgency. It would take years of inner work with Iya Osunnike, Baba ji Koleoso and the Institute of Whole Life Healing community, along with healing, release and understanding before that rage energy I carried was transmuted and cleared.

## It's In The DNA!

The reconnection with my biological father, a kindred spirit, was the catalyst that set me on the path to self-discovery and to ultimately find the Institute of Whole Life Healing. Our reunion was a missing puzzle piece we both needed to assist in our ongoing evolution as individuals and as light leaders. We will continue our beautiful cosmic dance and we are looking forward to more adventures to come! It is our mission to bring healing light to humanity, as our shared legacy for our children, grandchildren, great-grandchildren, and generations beyond! Light leader is definitely in the DNA!

# Priestess AyoDeji & Her Dad, Ralph L. Stevenson

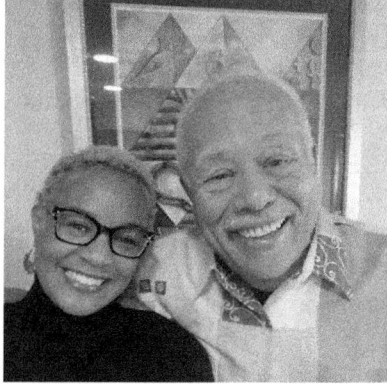

Lisa "AyoDeji" Allen is the first-born child for both of her parents. She was born in Brooklyn, New York and raised in Philadelphia, Pennsylvania. She has a degree in English from Lincoln University. On the metaphysical side, she is passionate about all things mystical and helping others find their light. She is a natural empath and her favorite spiritual tools include tarot, crystals and numerology. She may be reached at Sirian1111@gmail.com.

Ralph L. Stevenson was born and raised in Philadelphia, Pennsylvania. He is AyoDeji's father and an educator specializing in cultural awareness, the Ancient Nile Valley Civilization and Universal Law. He has the uncanny ability to bring light to the darkest places. His commitment to helping humanity raise its consciousness and recognize its own divinity is unwavering. His mantra is, "We are the ones we have been waiting for." And, we are indeed! Mr. Stevenson may be reached at belovenow@verizon.net.

# Know Thyself Series

## Etoke Fuatabong Lekeanju Atabong

Who am I? What am I? Why am I? How am I?

In this "KNOW THYSELF" series of poems, Chief Fuatabong Lekeanju Fonsa Etoke elaborates in verse, his subjective responses to the above questions. He is sharing with each and all of you, his unique and personal perspectives and story through the use of mythic references and metaphors.

In all religions and schools of spiritual development, the student is encouraged to know as much as they can about their very own unique self and what it means to have a human experience. With prolific use of metaphors, which stretch the limitations of language, the reader is going to be challenged and invited to introspect and exemplify from their experience, their personal responses, in their own words to the famous maxim "KNOW THYSELF".

# Wealth Substance Opulence and Abundance

I am wealth
POSSESSING
All of the Gifts
That God and nature have given to man
For right use.

I am wealth
ACCEPTING
Myself as I am
Favoured, Treasured, Bountiful, Beautiful
Complete and Victorious

I am wealth
OVERCOMING
All obstacles in the path
Of celebrating my life and my work in accordance
To my true self

I am wealth
EXPERIENCING
Fulfilment that comes in ordinary ways
From the earnest pursuit of God's will
In my life.

MAGNIFICENT WEALTH, I AM.
I am the Wealth already perfected in my world, of every
constructive thing,
I could possibly conceive of or decree.

---------

I am substance
APPLYING
My skills, resources, and talent
Uniquely in the service of God's will
In this physical realm

I am substance
QUESTING
My unfolding path
By fixing my attention with full DETERMINATION
On ETERNAL TRUTH

I am substance
PERFECTING
The powerful influence that I have
Over all substance and energy through my ability
to resonate with the forces of nature.

I am substance
COMPOUNDING
The purest essence of my inner being
With infinite SPIRITSELF within and without
Toward sacred ascension

MARVELLOUS SUBSTANCE, I AM
I am the Substance already perfected in my world, of every
constructive thing,
I could possibly conceive of or decree.

---------

I am opulence
EXUDING
Regal majesty
From tranquil and centred inner space
Enfolding beauteous soul

I am opulence
RADIATING
The eternal sparkling spirit-light
From the inner depth of my reverent life stream
Toward the cosmos and beyond

I am opulence

PULSATING
My three-pronged stellar flame
Brandishing its bubbly effervescence of magnetic vibrations
Within a beloved shrouded core

I am opulence
RESONATING
The sacred space of my vessel's
Exuberant bohemian magnificence with gusto
In multitudes of phases and arenas

SCINTILLATING OPULENCE, I AM.
I am the Opulence already perfected in my world, of every
constructive thing,
I could possibly conceive of or decree.

----------

I am abundance
COMMANDING
Comprehension of ultimate life mysteries
Toward ecstatic revelations of the unity of all
With nuanced paradoxes and conundrums

I am abundance
EXCELLING
In impossible tests and unbearable lessons
Marching forward eye deep in the conscious experience of each
moment
Participating, transmuting, and transcending

I am abundance
DEMONSTRATING
The wisdom of inspiriting
My exuberant human trajectory in this-here place and time
Within harmonious resplendent community living

I am abundance
EVOLVING
In ascension-bound glorious celebration heaven on earth while
manifesting
the divine destiny of self-fulfilment
For myself and for all.

FULFILLED ABUNDANCE I AM
I am the Abundance, already perfected in my world, of every
constructive thing,
I could possibly conceive of or decree.

# Light, Wisdom, Power, Love

I AM LIGHT
The radiance of LIGHT is glowing
Within every cell and atom of my body,
Bursting through my skin into the energy field
That surrounds my nominal, phenomenal, and other bodies;
Scintillating brilliantly beyond the crystal armour shield,
Which encapsulates me with invulnerable protection,
And prevents all but the righteous, positive, and good
From permeating my sacred space of light;
My light which repels darkness
With persistent brightness
Thus attracting other light
For the love of light
By knowing light,
By serving light,
By being light;
This light of GOD
That never fails.
I AM LIGHT
Receiving
Greater and Greater
LIGHT

I AM WISDOM
Totally, consciously aware
Of everything that I need to know
Through multidimensional omniscience
Having dropped the scales of perception
From my inner, outer, and phenomenal eyes
Having circumcised my subtle inner and outer ears
Having beheld the majesty of eternal truth that I quest
Having accepted the gifts that GOD and nature have given
To man for right use;
With WISDOM,
I integrate
In this now-time of furious change,
The sacred knowledge of ancient past,

And zooming panorama of impending future
With the in-depth awareness of this-here-self
And the out-there-infinity of cosmic boundlessness
Into this dynamic NOW of ageless time,
Toward
Co-creative accomplishments in the permanent present,
Surrendered to the loving will of GOD
Synchronized with the unfolding
Of his GREAT WISE PLAN.
I AM WISDOM
Acquiring
Greater and greater
WISDOM


I AM POWER
The momentous generator
Of power within
Propelling magnetized vortices
Of co-creative decrees
In resonance with
The source of generativity beyond,
Toward the manifestation of perfection,
Fuelling the exultant flares of the three-pronged flame
Intention, Direction, Manifestation ... Father, Son, Holy Ghost
The potent blue lightening of cosmic fire, Holy Ghost fire
With fierce awesome application of divine potency
Arcing from the laser sword of the divine warrior
Invincible intensity of the seven solar salvoes
Eviscerating, destroying, and transforming
Mis-education, mayhem, manipulation
Gaining victory over all imperfection
Opening the way to ASCENSION
I AM THE POWER,
Of the sacred-fire-directing
Intelligence of GOD
I AM POWER
Rightly using
Greater and greater
POWER

I AM LOVE
The passion of love
Saturating every thought, word, and deed
Counteracting rampant limitation
Obliterating imprudence and intolerance
With instructive unconditional loving comprehension
Of the lessons and tests
Encoded in the drama of life
Unfolding within this physical realm
Its ubiquitous paradoxes and conundrums
Of divine design;
This drama
Co-created and enacted
By diverse unseen forces and us;
Primal love
The ultimate winner
Over non-loving other forces
Claims complete victory within me
Making me a magnificent essence of love;
Of self ... a lover I AM
Of the other ... a lover I AM
Of my sistren ... a lover I AM
Of my brethren ... a lover I am
Of positive life forms ... a lover I AM
Of plants and animals ... a lover I AM
Of the expanding cosmos ... a lover I am
I AM LOVE
Experiencing
Greater and greater
LOVE

# SANCTIFIED SENSUOUS SEVEN DIRECTIONS

I celebrate my
SANCTIFIED SENSUOUS SEVEN directions by ....

Mining the direction of earth mother BELOW
I CONSUME the bounty of the precious sensational resources
From the generous bowels of this-here physical plane
Grounding me within a dynamic present dimensional essence

Soaring toward the sky father direction ABOVE,
I TRANSCEND via my boundless trajectory
Resplendent with hard-won mercurial fulfilment
Buoyantly experiencing the potency of ascendant ecstasy

Studying the direction to the NORTH,
I ACKNOWLEDGE all that there was, is, and will be
My finiteness, infinity, all paradoxes, all conundrums, and
The enigma of my embodiment in this physical dimension

Observing the direction to the SOUTH,
I BEHOLD the inner experience of the bounty of my bio-psychic
vessel
This insatiable life stream exploring the limited physical domain
In a self-imposed quest with obscure goals of spiritual edification

Embracing the sun-rising direction to the EAST
I MANIFEST the full spectrum of the rising sun's solar splendor
Radiating the plenitudes of my tangible and intangible gifts
Thus empowering my multi-dimensional divine infinity

Re-examining the sun-setting direction to the WEST,
I ENACT the objectives of my EARTH-PLANE INCARNATION
Consecrating my unique contribution to the unfolding of the
universal plan
As a LIVING TESTIMONIAL to my co-creative mission

Meditating on the unwavering direction of the CENTRE
I AM ENLIGHTENED by the mystic middle intersecting aperture,

That codifies the entire cosmic drama within me,
As it unfathomably propagates in the boundless beyond
Instructed by my senses and in these ways,
Do I celebrate
My SANCTIFIED SENSUOUS SEVEN directions.

# The One

Can I chant into ecstasy, like the monk?
...Who is "THE ONE" ... chanting?
Can I meditate into bliss, like the yogi?
...Who is "THE ONE" ... meditating?
Can I dance into trance, like the shaman?
...Who is "THE ONE" ... dancing?
Can I theoretically unify the universe, like the kabbalist?
...Who is "THE ONE" ... unifying?
Can I manipulate substance phenomenally, like the alchemist?
...Who is "THE ONE" ... manipulating?
Can I perceive Eternal Truth, like the mystic?
...Who is "THE ONE" ... perceiving?
Can I comprehend the cosmos, like the sage?
...Who is "THE ONE" ... comprehending?
Can I write poetry of mystery, like the sufist?
...Who is "THE ONE" ... writing?

I would know,
When I know
Who "THE ONE" is.

# Chief Fuatabong Lekeanju Fonsa Etoke

In addition to writing poetry, Chief Fuatabong Lekeanju Fonsa Etoke is an award-winning wood sculptor, a designer of African couture, a musician, a dancer, a shaman, and a jewelry maker. Growing up in the rain forest where the Fako Mountain slopes into the Atlantic Ocean in Cameroon, Africa, he was immersed in the rich and organic interplay of traditional arts and culture with cosmopolitan influences from around the world.

His combination of a voracious quest for knowledge and experience as well as his love of language led the young student of life into private journaling and poetry writing, from which we have chosen a sample to share with the world. In this selection of poems, which reflect on the fundamental questions of human existence, he takes time out of his professional responsibilities as a Civil Engineer and other responsibilities as a traditional ruler to explore in verse our shared human identity within a spiritually inspired perspective.

For life enrichment and to participate in the renaissance of the heritage and culture of Africa, Chief Fuatabong Lekeanju Fonsa Etoke may be reached via email at: afipartners2@gmail.com.

# Ancestral Pillars of my Soul
## Makhosi Yeye Gogo Nana Omari

In a desire that you will find spiritual inspiration, I open the curtains of my personal window sharing a very small, yet significant portion of my spiritual growth process, including some work I have done for others.

Awakening to your higher self can be an arduous and confusing time. Especially, when you sense something invisible consistently has a negative impact on your path. This, too, was my experience. Prior to gaining mastery over this force, my narrative led me through several layers of spiritual cleansing, initiations, and finally to a profound, undeniable connection with my indigenous ascended ancestors. Their presence affirmed me as a radiant lovelight vessel, a mystical being, divine teacher, spiritual light leader, and most importantly, that I was not insane.

One of the preeminent gifts passed down to me, through my SAYU (Sangoma, Akan, Yoruba, Universal Light) priesthood initiations, is assisting others in clearing spiritual interferences. Your ancestors are a key factor and component for repairing simple to more complex issues in your life. Not just you but anyone in this world can feel cut off from their ancestral lineage with no guidance on how to repair it.

My ascended ancestors offer their healing modalities activated in my SAYU and through Ubunye Sangoma Indigenous Priesthood School (UBSA). Entering these portals deepens your spiritual journey, infuses your ancestral connections, and helps align you to your destined path.

https://www.ubunyesangoma.org/

Have you ever wondered why there are certain topics that are not addressed in the normal status quo of society? There could be a plethora of reasons, such as social taboos, belief systems, spiritual differences, lack of tangible proof, and the list definitely continues.

On your journey of uncovering a deeper purpose for the authentic self, there are objects that must be propelled into nothingness prior to securing a relaxing seat in the shade of the sacred Baobab Tree. My seat was finally claimed after undergoing an arduous spiritual process of turning the soil of the earth to get to the roots of my sacred ancestral tree. Once your ancestral roots are revealed, there is an unshakeable magnetic field that pulls you towards the best parts of who you are and who they are. You are the temple where your ancestors reside and cannot be anything outside of the chromosomes of your DNA structure.

*This conscious intertwining mends your evolving soul through the duration of this earthly expedition towards a more pristine experience.*

# Uniqueness of The Journey

While entering the darkness of the cave, listen intently, you can hear the sound from the crackling firewood which provides, not only a calming light, but an equitable amount of comfort to offset any chill that may be felt. As you settle into this space, our collective ancestors become excited and reveal themselves in the colorful hues of the dancing flames.

On the cavern walls, we witness huge individual ancestral shadow figures. Their distinct, exotic patterns of uninhibited motions are captivating. These syncopated movements by our indigenous ancestors, shadow dancers, gradually, become synchronized to the beating pattern of each of our hearts. As we open our eyes, we are puzzled as to when they actually became closed. The dim light, given off by a love infused fire, suddenly becomes brighter as we telepathically agree to dance in the uniqueness of the venerated company of our indigenous worldwide ancestral lineages.

The uniqueness of your spiritual journey is yours alone. There is no one who can measure the positive or the gloom-ridden impact it has on your life. In order for elevation, transformation, and conscious living to occur there must be acknowledgement that spiritual laws exist in our universe governed by a Supreme energy.

Once this is acknowledged, you do your best to learn what they are, practice them and live in the frequency of your authentic self. Simple as this may sound, when standing in my Lovelight presence, you would never know the intricate and grueling processes I sustained to be in this exuberant space. I was met with many obstacles, however the ones that were most prevalent and difficult to navigate were invisible negative forces.

Called by many names, these malevolent spirits were never frightening to me, nevertheless, I did feel maddened by the vulnerability of their forced presence. It seized a precious portion of my younger adult years causing immense physical, mental, and emotional impairment. I later began to comprehend spiritual warfare was actually in existence and my ancestral pantheons were on the front line assertive and unyielding. Eventually, with their effectual presence, power, and my openness to something never taught, I was able to rid myself from the harness of unholy spirits.

As significant as my encounters seem, they cannot take the place or fulfill the requirements of things yet to be unfolded in your personal cave with your ancestors. As we take this journey together, may whatever needs to be decoded for your further ascension and exploration of your soul, be revealed by your ancestors in a gentle and manageable manner. Regardless of your ethnicity or spiritual platform, your ancestors are guardians, unique healers, ascended masters, protectors willing to support your spiritual growth wherever you landed. At any point in your life that you begin to feel as if you are stuck in a wet patch of concrete, may the memory of this sharing serve as cool water that dissolves the cement until you can once again, freely move and spread your unique wings.

# The Gift of Spiritual Connections

As you push through the places of difficulty the ancestors will bring people into your life to help you through. This is how I met Queen Mother Osunnike of the Institute of Whole Life Healing. She was single at the time and I was on the last leg of clearing one nagging aggressive negative spirit from my energetic field. Over thirty years ago, we were attending an Akan Akom Ceremony. This is an African Indigenous healing ceremony from Ghana, West Africa, where the Abosom/deities come to bless and heal people. During this time I was already an Akan Priest. I was sitting next to Iya and my ancestors told me she was my teacher. I turned to her, and I said, "You're my teacher," she then turned to me and said, "I know." Thereafter we returned and continued our focus on the ceremony. Queen Mother Osunnike eventually became my Reiki master and was very instrumental in helping me to rid myself of the final invasive spirit.

I met Priest King Baba Koleoso when Iya surprised me by stopping in my home in Baltimore for a brief visit. Baba Koleoso was kind, gentle and had a strong presence. I noticed how he had a sincere interest in sharing wisdom with my sons and even gifted them a book of his powerful teachings. Their energy together felt magnetic and just right. They became the family of Light Leader Elders that I trusted for most of my personal spiritual consultations.

Over the next couple of years, both witnessed my ancestors guide me to unexpected pathways. Not only did my ancestors lead me to the path of becoming a Sangoma Priestess, indigenous healers of South Africa, but also an Orisha Priestess, Indigenous healers of Nigeria, West Africa. I felt very connected to the "Many Paths One Truth" that the Institute of Whole Life Healing upholds, as this is exactly how my path unfolded. It made sense that we would develop a long-standing spiritual relationship, honoring each other's gifts and referring clients where we deemed necessary.

*In this moment our ancestors have gifted you and I with this spiritual connection may we use it wisely.*

# Healing Roots for Better Fruit

Healing my roots for better fruit was done with an awareness of the fact that my roots were invaded by harmful spirit substances. The results of invasive negative spirit tapping left me emotionally drained, out of sorts, and very disconsolate. My body needed a cup of soothing tea, yet my hands were too weak to accept the invitation from my mind to pour the boiling water from the singing teapot. Meanwhile, I was slowly watching life disappear into a foggy midst. In spite of every dark thing, each step on my path led me closer to being healed. Through this misty fog, my ancestors showed up guiding me through a gradual clearing process. The deep cleansing steps that followed did not happen overnight. It was years before I eliminated the destructive ones. I went from a touring performing arts entertainer to a recluse with the turmoil tucked away inside me.

In order to heal your roots for better fruits, you first must be honest and want the healing. Take time to observe yourself for signs and symptoms of negative spiritual attachments. Some symptoms, to name a few, may include feeling like someone is touching you when you are sleeping. Being pinned down, unable to move when you are awake. Hearing loud sounds from various types of instruments that are more like noise than music. Whispering voices mumbling incoherent words. Awakening to red marks and scratches on your body, and the ultimate, sexual violation or intrusion.

I want to be clear that this is different from someone suffering from a mental health challenge. Spiritual treatment does not, by any means, take care of or replace any medical treatments. Yes, it can sometimes be difficult to distinguish between the two. Either way, it is important to know and acknowledge which one you need at that point in your life.

When you have a spiritual diagnosis, we do what is necessary to ameliorate the symptoms. Please understand that this is not a heuristic process. How long it takes depends on the circumstances and the willingness of you to "trust the process." In working with others who experience negative spirit attachments, I take them through a specific spiritual diagnostic procedure guided by my ancestors to identify the root of the attached spirit: be it an unsettled ancestor, entity, or foreign spirit.

My ancestors instructed me to review my childhood for all the good memories and then all the not so good memories. I recalled, I was very quiet and always content to be close to my mother. Playing with my sister and two male cousins, who were like siblings, was a fun time. One day we took turns sitting on my mother's knitted blanket where we each got a chance to ride while the other person pulled the blanket running as fast as they could down our long hallway. Being pulled on the splintery wood grain floor, we would stretch our arms along the narrow walls just enough to keep from falling off the blanket or bumping into the wall.

For some reason pulling out the splinters from the blanket and our skin was just as fun as riding on it. Even though my mother was working hard using a metal washboard with wooden trimming to scrub our laundry in the bathtub, the best part of this memory was seeing her in my peripheral every time I slid by on her blanket. At this point I had no worries and definitely not any recognizable spiritual interferences. Undoubtedly, a great memory.

After this fun review, I went to the database of my mind and pulled all the files I labeled as "bad memories." I found what made these files cohesive. This process helped me to pinpoint the when, the where, the how and the by whom negative spirits were deposited on me. The onset and recognizing of some of my symptoms happened in my early adult years; however, in my work with some clients, the onset and recognizing of symptoms did not occur until their later adult years. They had great childhood experiences, and this yielded great childhood adult memories.

In adulthood, negative spiritual attachments can be transmitted at any time and in different ways. They can be transmitted generationally, through current marriages, partnerships, previous lifetime agreements, being in a place where bad energy resides, physically touching others who carry bad spirits. A prime example is in the movie *Fallen* where Denzel Washington chases the spirit of a criminal who was executed, but keeps transferring his negative spirit to different people through touch. Whether attachments occur in childhood or adult life it's important to recognize them and work to have them released from your life force field.

*My goal is to ensure you stand firmly planted in the soil of your ancestral footprints, as a strong unshakeable tree healing roots for better fruit.*

# Managing Interferences

Over the years, I have counseled and provided spiritual assistance for all types of people with all types of negative spirits. Some had spiritual husbands from past lives who were upset that they were not part of their current lives. Issues are also created when a baby is aborted and continues to cling to their parents. Couples who have miscarriages, stillbirths, or SID could be dealing with negative spiritual interferences. Homes that have not been cleansed can hold bad spirits. Someone had a deceased father who continued with harassment in their dream space.

Another person was beaten by both deceased parents, the bad spirit passed to them creating hostile and volatile behavior. One client had ancestors who owned slaves, and made the client treat others from that perspective. In another case, a person was bothered by their ancestors who were part of the apartheid regime. Their ancestors were upset because their descendants would not acknowledge them. The person did not want to take on the guilt and shame of sharing blood with those that took part in a cruel system; acknowledgement was mandatory so that the cleansing could take place.

Regardless of the pain you feel, you must get to the poison at the root of your tree so the weed that is strangling it can be extracted. Now space is created for oxygen and water to flow more easily into your soil upon your roots. This ensures your tree continues to grow towards the sun unhindered.

Every spirit, good and bad ones, need to be handled according to how they are showing up in your life. Managing interference comes with knowing when a spirit has ill intent and is causing trouble in your life. Open up your heart to receive a solution. Having an expert guide you through this journey is, in most cases, necessary for spiritual attachments to be broken.

*Acknowledging the apple is sweet and the seed is poisonous is a wise decision.*

# Moving Towards the Light

In order to move towards the light, I take you through divination also called "spiritual reading." If you are unfamiliar with divination, when you sit with not only me but my divine spirits. I proceed to find out why your ancestors brought you to me, what is going on with you, what is going on with your ancestors, and what needs may need resolving for your spiritual alignment and balance. Afterwards, if needed I provide a spiritual prescription.

Every person is different, and the spiritual remedies are based on your circumstances of what your ancestors may be requesting, any negative spiritual attachments and other issues that need adjusting. There is not a cookie cutter remedy. As a Spiritual Doctor, I give you a spiritual prescription that you should follow if you want to have success. If there is anything else needed after the spiritual prescription follow up, such as rites of passage, initiations, a series of cleansings, ancestral shadow work, or other spiritual processes, I will share that with you, and you make a decision concerning what happens next.

Wanting to find your spiritual gifts and align yourself with your ancestors require some portals to close and some to open. Closing the ones that are doorways for negative spirits and opening the portals to your elevated divine ancestors. Sometimes it is just a matter of releasing one's ego.

Some of the darkest spirits feed off the ego, which can be one of the most difficult attachments for people to let go of. Once I assist you in recognizing the damage your ego is causing and the willingness is there for letting go, the process of elevation begins. Washing away of all the stagnation that has been built up over the years. Getting the proper spiritual dialysis to purify your spirit is vital. The awakening to ancestral healing is felt in your bloodstream and your lymphatic system making your spiritual vessel ready to align with the LIGHT.

*It is in your bones where we live in the LIGHT.*

# The Calling

The path to the unknown can be challenging or too hair-raising, due to unconsciousness and improper teachings. Through this indigenous healing process, ascended ancestral calling, every student is guided to their teacher by their ancestors. When you come to me, and you say you have a calling it has to be verified through a specific formula passed down through indigenous healing cultures. Once I verify that the ancestral protocols and procedures are in place for the calling, I become your Gobela, Makhosi, Baba, Nana, or Yeye depending on the path you are destined for.

When I received my calling to become a Sangoma, I had never heard of it and did not want to do it as I was already an established Akan Priestess. Long story short, I got the ukuthwasa sickness. This happens when you are called by your ancestors and do not get well until you answer the call. I lost my ability to walk and ended up laying in one spot or crawling.

Then one night I had a visit from a female ancestor dressed with a crown on her head, cloth that Sangomas wear, medicine pouches on both her triceps and holding a shaker in her right hand. She stared at me for a while and then said, "You must come home and answer your call."

I asked, "If I answer, will I get better?"

She replied, "Yes," and this is when I truly surrendered to my process. While I was actually undergoing my ukuthwasa training, Oshun, goddess of the river, came and claimed me as her daughter. Once again, I did not want to go through any more initiations. I recalled how complicated my life got by rejecting my previous calling and I dare not say no to Yeye Oshun. Ironically, my father had his DNA Ancestry tested and I found out I had ancestry from all three paths that I received my calling to. This proves our ancestors are the integration of all of who we are.

*The Calling takes you to places picking up pieces of yourself, your ancestral pantheon, bringing them home to remember who you are.*

## Surrendering To Your Ancestral Pantheon

Traditionally, our Ancestors are called by numerous names including, Egungun, Nsamanfo, and Amadlozi. In my humble opinion, knowing your personal ancestral pantheon is something that should be an automatic thing in this life. However, getting to know who they are and how they function is an amazing process. Your ancestral pantheon is not only your ancestors, but the elevated beings they carry with them. These elevated spirits are ones who your ancestors were initiated to and worked with in family and spiritual matters when they were alive on this earth.

The spiritual gifts are passed down. You may be next in line to pick up your healing stick. This calling in the family cannot be ignored or avoided. They will make certain the medicine is carried on and healing work continues. Everyone in the family has a chosen one and sometimes not just one but several family members are chosen by their ancestors to carry on and remember the sacred ways. You are the seed to ensure ancestral medicine thrives in the here and now. When your ancestral pantheons are near or working in your life there are major shifts and transmissions. When these transmissions take place you feel pure love, an unshakable excitement about their presence, your entire being is lighter.

Being in the presence of ascended ancestors is when your spirit is most balanced. You will discover something about yourself that you did not know. The journey with them will, absolutely, not look like the way you thought. Let go and surrender all expectations.

*Surrendering to your ancestral pantheon will only lead you to the healing truth until sweet surrender is a way of life.*

## One Self In the One Nest

Ascended ancestors are not in the great beyond. They are right next to you whispering, guiding, and departing their wisdom. They are living in your solar plexus, consuming the same foods, and letting you know which are taboo. They are the healing steam from your hot bath. The purifying waters in your cold shower. They are the magnetic pull to your choice of home living and travel. The colors you want to wear are their colors. Your facial expressions are the same as your greatest grandmothers and greatest grandfathers. They move through mountains to help you move mountains. Their voices speak in the wind and their hands are the breeze. Your shoulders shimmy from the chill. They are the nature that nurtures your spirit. They reign on the earth with rain drops of wisdom that the stars granted to them many moons ago. Your ascended ancestors are the jewels embedded in you. You can, in fact, pluck them from the epidermis of your skin, receiving hidden gems of your consciousness.

*Ascended Ancestors are the connective tissue in our roots, owners of our cells, steering us to our true selves, from the one nest of our bloodline to the oneness in the universe, while graciously serving as the sacred pillars for our soul's ascension.*

# Makhosi Yeye Gogo Nana
# (Dr. Aminah Elana Omari)

Makhosi Yeye Gogo Nana, Dr. Aminah Elana R. Omari was born in Hartsville, South Carolina, and grew up in Baltimore, Maryland. While working as professional modern and ballet dancer she received her calling into the African Indigenous Priesthood connecting for Akan, Sangoma, and Yoruba traditions. She is a Reiki master, with certifications in Massage Therapy, Foot Reflexology, Kinesiology and Kemetic Yoga. She holds a PhD in Philosophy and Metaphysical Ministry. The founder of the first Sangona School in the US, she is a pioneer for Sangoma practices in the states. Graduates of her lineage are found throughout the US, making it more accessible for people in America and the Diaspora to recognize and experience the potency of Indigenous Ancestral practices.

Through the mastery of divination, she provides guidance for healing of ancestral and other spiritual issues. She is featured in Crazywise, a documentary film, addressing the connection between ancestors and mental health illness. She is also a featured author in the book Iyanifa: Woman of Wisdom. She enjoys sharing the healing practices of Nichieren Buddhism and Agniholtra.

ubunyesangoma@gmail.com

# Whispers of My Ancestors
## Regina Abegunde Harris

This story is not just about me; it's about the resilient spirit of the human soul and the beauty of community support. The love that I have for my godparents, Iya Osunnike and Baba Koleoso, and how they embodied my family tradition and helped me heal myself and to hear the whispers of my ancestors once again.

In this chapter, I am sharing my journey of self-discovery, empowerment, and living in alignment with my deepest truths. For within every struggle, there lies the potential for profound growth, and within every ancestral whisper, the possibility of a harmonious balance. I'm sharing with each and all of you what it means to listen as I heard the call to becoming a priestess of the Sacred Feminine Mysteries and my Orisha/deity Eshu/Elegba who represents the crossroads. Through this process my mind is happily reexploring with you my ancestors whispering, "Do you know who you are?"

Finally, I said yes, and over the years I have come to embrace my spiritual gifts while honoring the wisdom of my ancestors and their stories. You see, I strive to leave a legacy not only for my children but also for all those who seek a deeper connection to their ancestral roots and a greater understanding of their purpose. As a Sacred Spiritual Light Leader, I share my story; may it resonate with those of you on your own journeys of healing and transformation. Now, I invite you to listen to the Whispered Echoes of YOUR Ancestors.

# When Ancestral Honoring
# Through Family Traditions Began

Our family paid tribute to our ancestors in various ways. Growing up, elders prepared me to be a custodian of those who crossed over and raised me to honor the dead. It was hot the summer of 1985, and I was nine years old when I was first told that I would be helping to decorate the graves. It was a time when family members would return home to honor the dead. I had two long black pigtails, and my Momma Edna made me a white dress that fit perfectly for this special occasion. I always loved staying at my great grandmother's house. Her home was incredibly beautiful and full of tradition and history. I had never met my great great grandfather, but he left us a legacy of the importance of taking care of the dead as a co-founder of the black cemetery.

In continuing his legacy, my Grandmother Young maintained a beautiful farm and sacred space for the family. On this land, we fed ourselves and others in the community. There were pear trees and apple trees. The house was adorned with coneflowers, day lilies, cosmos, sunflowers, azaleas, hibiscus, white lilac, rose of Sharon, and honeysuckles. She had a knack for reusing things and had me gather items from the back kitchen to prep for decorating the graves. I could sit anywhere in the house and look at the splendid flowers, trees, and bluegrass. It was always such a serene place to be.

Visiting the graves was not to be rushed; there was plenty of time. This day was significant for all of us. Grandmother Young would send me outside to fetch an empty bottle, which we filled with hot water, dishwashing liquid, and a teaspoon of Pine-Sol so that we could clean our ancestors' headstones. And close out the ceremony with flowers, a song, or a good story about them.

We retreated from the gravesites to a house filled with the smell of food being freshly prepared. My Aunt Dorothy allowed me to assist with the cooking. I felt so grown up, putting on my own apron from my grandmother's drawer. The kitchen was always buzzing with conversation among the women, and I had learned to stay quiet. I understood the importance of keeping kitchen discussions a secret from an incredibly young age. At the dinner table, we would sit and tell stories and songs of our departed loved ones. We put together a menu of the favorite dishes of those who were no longer with us. This would include fried chicken and fish, greens, mac and cheese, okra, stuffing, sweet potatoes, corn, potato salad, black-eyed peas, and squash.

As the years progressed, my great-grandmother was no longer tilling the land. She had begun to share many of her responsibilities and insights with me. It felt like the transition from fall to winter, with her energy gradually fading. During this period, she started teaching me about compassion, love, and respect for the land and the community. This stage of her life, which she often referred to as the "fall stage," revealed a gentle and nurturing side of her that I warmly welcomed.

As we tended to the graves and the land, I discovered that my gift was something connected to honoring our ancestral history and legacy. Something was being passed down to me. My great-grandmother would soon transition and losing the safety net of her loving home caused this gift to be interrupted. I stopped listening because now it felt like I was in a nightmare.

## Meeting Baba a Year After the Transition of Grandmother Young

However, my ancestors continued looking out for me even though I didn't realize it at the time. I had turned my back on my family simply because I did not seem to fit in anywhere or belong, and the lack of my biological father made the world feel unkind and cruel. But then my community dad, Mfundi (Elder Don Offutt), who always made sure I was properly looked out for and protected introduced me to Baba. Next thing I knew, in the corridors of time, my journey intersected with a man of extraordinary wisdom and grace – Baba Nashid "Koleoso" Fakhrid-Deen. His towering presence shaped not just my understanding of life but also the very fabric of what would become our tight-knit community.

What lingers most vividly in my memory is Baba's candid discourse on life's nuances, particularly his sincere guidance to us young ladies about the challenges we might face. On the University of Kentucky Campus, he was a distinguished figure, navigating the grounds with a large box of papers and a projector perched on top. Clad in a captivating blend of modern and African attire, his style mirrored his timeless elegance. Baba's aura exuded confidence and charisma, leaving an indelible mark on the campus landscape.

Yet, beyond his impeccable exterior, Baba was a scholar, an intellect that resonated with humility and compassion. He carried with him a wealth of knowledge, not just academically but in the intricate tapestry of life. He championed the importance of higher education, fostering a sense of community that became a haven for us to share our joys and struggles.

As a community mentor and father figure, Baba's unique insights reached not only the young women but also the men, guiding them on how to carry themselves around us. He wasn't just a teacher; he embodied the essence of a father figure, imparting lessons on what to seek in a good man. His teachings resonated so profoundly that I credit him as the reason I found my husband.

In the beginning, most of the community were men and somethings Baba just couldn't provide for the young ladies. He would always say we needed a "Sacred Feminine" woman for our guidance. The universe heard him and delivered to him our Queen Mother "Iya Osunnike" who later became his loving wife and co-founder of the Institute of Whole Life Healing. As a result, I began embarking on a transformative journey, starting with setting up an ancestor altar, a connection to the spiritual realm that I had long neglected. In seeking guidance from my community of seers within the Institute, I discovered not only a path to personal empowerment but also a collective movement towards healing and wholeness.

# Meeting Iya Osunnike

In the sacred enclave of a friend's house, a gathering of spiritual minds unfolded, bringing together Daundra, Crystal, and a circle of other remarkable women. The ambiance was an ethereal symphony, with dim lights casting a mystical glow and an enchanting fragrance that filled the room. Uncertain of what awaited a blend of excitement and nervous anticipation permeated the air.

As I stepped into this space, my senses were immediately heightened. In the corner, amidst the soft hum of conversations, sat a woman whose beauty transcended the physical realm. Her eyes, a deep honey hue, seemed to penetrate beyond the surface, connecting with the very essence of my soul. Every movement she made was a dance of grace, a deliberate choreography in sync with cosmic forces. Yet, it wasn't merely her physical allure that captivated me; it was the profound compassion emanating from her being.

In her presence, one could sense the ancient, the timeless wisdom woven into her existence. She spoke with a depth that echoed the mysteries of the universe, declaring that this wisdom resided within each of us. A transformative energy enveloped the room, and as she spoke, a simultaneous fear and awe gripped my heart. Meeting her was like encountering a force beyond comprehension.

# Sick and Tired of Living in Distress

The ancestral whispers began to haunt my nights. Picture a time when my husband, a priest of Obatala (i.e., a man of exceptional divine love and light), walked beside me through the dark shadows of my fears and insecurities. Every little event seemed to trigger me, causing me pain, but instead of communicating my feelings, I would hold them in and act out my pain. The incessant other worldly chatter played like an ethereal symphony that kept me awake, scared, and in a perpetual state of unrest. To silence these spirits, I made the television my nightly companion, white noise drowning out the mysterious messengers that sought to communicate as I drifted into sleep. For years, this ritual persisted, and my husband shared our bed with the glow of the TV. My husband, a pillar of love and patience, had stood by me through the tumultuous years of our relationship, marked by my inability to sleep without the TV on. This wasn't just about my struggle; it was a call to heal the ancestral patterns that gripped my family.

Soon, a journey of awakening, embracing the Wisdom of Ancestral Healing in the quiet solitude of a bathroom, locked away from the world, I found myself at a crossroads, reminiscent of a childhood memory that had haunted my mother. As a child, I had spoken to spirits, a gift that scared her, leading her to push me to repress what she couldn't comprehend. Decades later, as a wife and mother, I was grappling with sleepless nights, trapped in a cycle of chatter that echoed throughout the darkness I had drowned out with the television's glow. The familiar bathroom floor became a symbolic space where the echoes of the past collided with the present.

Feeling stuck in a fog of misery and confusion, I confronted the stark reality of my life. Aggressiveness and competitiveness had become my armor, shielding the internal suffering that no one could see. Ready to face my truth, I called upon Iya Osunnike and Baba Koleoso for a reading. In those precious moments on the phone, they brought peace to my chaos and clarity to my insanity. The words, "You're not crazy, dear, you have been chosen by your ancestors to heal the generational pain" echoed inside my ears. You are able to hear the ancestors' words of wisdom, guidance and unity for healing the world...listen.

In that moment, I felt their presence with me, guiding me, and giving me strength and approval of what I was allowed to be a part of. I sensed their love and felt the weight of their sacrifices and the love they had for the community. It was a humbling experience, knowing that I had been chosen to carry on their legacy and continue the work they had started.

Now within the community of seers, and the visionary founders of the Institute of Whole Life Healers, this meeting marked a significant juncture in my journey. This powerful network, dedicated to spiritual growth and healing, became a sanctuary where the light of everyone could truly shine. The Institute reflected a convergence of kindred spirits, unified by a shared purpose to bring healing, guidance, and transformation to those seeking solace and enlightenment.

In the presence of these remarkable souls, I discovered a community where the mysteries of the spiritual realm were explored, and the path to healing and enlightenment was illuminated. It was a place where each unique light being contributed to collective brilliance, fostering a bond that transcended the mundane and embraced the extraordinary.

Guided by my godparents, I began the work of clearing and healing our bloodline. The first initiation, the Sacred Feminine Mysteries, was a purifying hands-on journey into my inner energy of divine femininity. Through this process, I found not only personal transformation but also a deep connection to a community that embraced my vulnerabilities.

As I reflect on the years my husband spent sleeping with the TV on, sacrificing his own peace for my comfort, I realized the magnitude of his love. My Sacred Feminine Mysteries initiation became a bridge to understanding how to begin unveiling my wisdom that had long been hidden.

In the embrace of ancestral healing, self-discovery, and community support, I stepped into a new chapter, breaking free from the chains that bound me and being there for those in need of my gifts. This is not just my story; it's a testament to the resilience of the human spirit and the power of doing the work, facing the truth, and operating from a place of love and compassion and the ancestral wisdom to guide us toward a brighter, more balanced future.

After completing my transformative healing journey with the Institute and under the guidance of my godparents, propound shifts occurred within me. As I emerged from this cocoon of self-discovery, I stepped into the world with newfound balance and wholeness, a testament to the power of healing and spiritual growth. What unfolded was a narrative of how my inherent gifts and the fiery essence within me were channeled to radiate love and compassion, warming the hearts of those around me as a reflection of the deep healing that had taken place within my soul.

Initially, as I embarked on this path, the brilliance of the lights before me seemed blinding. Nervousness, like a tremor, shook my already delicate frame. The desire to honor my ancestors and uphold the traditions passed down by my husband and myself amplified every emotion within me. Pride, gratitude, loss, and a profound appreciation for the community and those who walked the path before me swirled within, creating a kaleidoscope of sentiments.

The fire that lived within me was no longer a source of fear but a beacon of light, a guiding force that illuminated the path for those who sought solace and understanding. The blend of my ancestral heritage and the traditions passed down through generations became a tapestry of wisdom, woven into my interactions and contributions.

As I navigated this newfound balance and wholeness, it became evident that my journey was not solitary. It was a dance of interconnected souls, a symphony of healing, and a celebration of the collective strength of the community. I stood as a living testament to the transformative power of embracing one's true self and leveraging those gifts for the greater good.

In the radiance of my balanced leadership and the warmth of my compassionate fire, I continued to show up in the world, now a beacon of inspiration for those on their own paths of healing and self-discovery.

## This Little Light of Mine, I'm Going to Let it Shine

Yes, I was invited to open our annual ceremony. Surrounded by thousands of people from the community, we gathered on Dr. Martin Luther King Day to pay tribute to the great civil rights leader. The significance of the day added an extra layer of emotions to the already profound moment. As I looked out to a sea of faces, I could not help but to feel a deep connection to my ancestors and their struggles for justice and equality like Dr. King.

Baba had stood on this very stage in front of the community; explaining what the pouring of libations/holy water is and the gravity of its importance. The ceremony that my husband and son were about to perform was a libation also – a sacred ritual of honoring our ancestors. It was tradition that my "Baba" had carried out with my husband and both of our sons so many times before, when he was still with us on the physical plane. Now, here I stood. It was my turn to stand in my power and let my light shine. In that moment, I felt the ancestral presence with me, guiding me, and giving me strength and approval of what I was allowed to be a part of. I felt the weight of their sacrifices and the love they had for the community. It was a humbling experience, knowing that I had been chosen to carry on their legacy and continue the work they had started.

In the name of Dr. King, we poured the libations, offered prayers and words of gratitude to and for our ancestors. The words flowed from my heart, filled with love and reverence. The energy of the room shifted as everyone began calling out the names of their ancestral loved ones, who began to spiritually arrive, one by one. The energy of our ancestors was there, listening and blessing our gathering. Standing on that stage, and listening to the ancestral whispers, I began to feel a sense of purpose and a deep connection to something greater than myself. I knew that I was part of a lineage of change-makers, and it was my duty to carry that torch forward.

As I spoke, I could not help but feel a deep sense of love for my community. It was a love that has been passed down through generations, a love that had been nurtured and strengthened by the struggles and triumphs of those who came before us. In that moment, I realized the power of our collective history and the importance of honoring our ancestors – no matter what.

As the ceremony ended, I felt a sense of peace and fulfillment. I knew that I had honored my ancestors and my community in the best way I could. As I stepped off the stage, I carried with me a sense of renewal and purpose and a deep love for my heritage and the people who came before me.

# Holding Space for My Uncle

At another time, I made a choice about how to honor those who have crossed over during my uncle's funeral, and listened as he whispered what he would want me to say. As we all sat in silence, I went to the front to front to tell his story. In that moment, I had a knowing while standing in my power about honoring our ancestors. It was about me recognizing the strength and wisdom that they had passed down to us and using it to create positive change in our community. It was also about acknowledging the sacrifices they had made, the love they had for us and carrying that love forward in everything we do.

My uncle, who had been a pillar of strength and support for me throughout my life, had recently passed away while writing this chapter. As I drove to upstate New York, I was flooded with all the good times I had with my cousins. His first wife, (my aunt Geneva), had also passed away several years ago, leaving behind my cousins. This funeral was not only a time to mourn the loss of my uncle, but also a moment to bring together the different branches of our family and honor the love and connections that we all shared.

In my speech at the funeral. I spoke about the powerful love my Aunt Geneva and Uncle shared during the time they were together. I spoke about the love they had for family and how the power of that love and compassion could bridge divides and bring people closer together. I also shared how my uncle and aunt had been the epitome of a loving and supportive family, and how their example had shaped my understanding of what it meant to truly care for one another. Instead of allowing grief to divide us, I chose to use my role as a priestess to bring us closer together as I listened to my uncle on the other side, reminding us of the love that binds us as a family.

In front of my uncle's coffin, I felt his presence and my aunt, guiding me and giving me strength. I knew that they would have wanted us to come together in love and celebrate his life and honor his memory. I am grateful for the opportunity to have shown up in this way at my uncle's funeral, to have been a source of strength and support for my cousins and even his new wife. Listening to the wise voices of the ancient women in my family and absorbing their teachings on tending to our ancestors and their memories became the cornerstone of my spiritual journey. This unique training cultivated within me a profound sense of responsibility, sparking a deep commitment to community service and activism.

## Honoring the En-Slaved Ancestors

As my spiritual path deepened, I found myself transforming into an advocate for justice and equality. This commitment took a tangible form in my significant involvement in the removal of statues from Cheapside, a historic place that held layers of ancestral memories in Lexington, Kentucky. In this endeavor, I not only served as an activist but also had the privilege of engaging with the ancestors, offering them the respect and honor they deserved, often behind the scenes.

During my journey, Cheapside became a sacred space where the echoes of history met the fervor of contemporary activism. In the quiet moments, amidst the work of dismantling statues, I communed with the ancestors, listening to their stories, and acknowledging their enduring presence. It was a profound experience that underscored the vital importance of recognizing and honoring our ancestors, both within our local community and on an international scale.

This bridge in my journey illuminated the interconnectedness of honoring the past and shaping a more just future. The removal of several statues was not just about erasing symbols of oppression but about reclaiming a space for the voices of those who came before us. Eternally connected to the struggles and triumphs of those who paved the way for us to be FREE.

As I navigated this multifaceted role of activist and spiritual practitioner, I realized the profound impact that community service could have. The harmonious tapestry woven by listening to ancestral wisdom and advocating for justice became a guiding force in my life. Each step, whether in quiet reverence for the ancestors or in the forefront of activism, became a testament to the intricate dance of honoring the past while actively shaping the present and future.

As I stand at the culmination of this chapter, I reflect on the lessons learned, the trials overcome, and the profound connections forged.

The ancient women in my family, through their whispered teachings, laid the foundation for a unique spiritual journey. A journey that rippled outward, transforming me into an activist, a vessel for justice and equality. My involvement in the removal of statues from Cheapside was not merely an act of dismantling physical structures; it was a sacred communion with the ancestors, an acknowledgment of their stories, and a dedication to honoring their enduring spirits.

Cheapside became a canvas where the strokes of history met the brush of contemporary activism. In the quiet moments of reverence, as statues were disassembled, I conversed with the ancestors, ensuring their voices echoed in the spaces of remembrance. It was a profound reminder that our actions today are eternally connected to the struggles and triumphs of those who paved the way before us.

This chapter, illuminated by the warmth of ancestral fire and the beacon of community service, concludes not as an ending but as a transition to the next phase of this transformative odyssey. As I step into the future, I carry with me the sacred responsibility to continue nurturing the flame of justice, equality, and ancestral honor.

May this story be more than just a personal narrative; may it serve as an inspiration for those who stand at the crossroads of their own journeys. May it be a testament to the power of embracing one's true self, of advocating for what is just, and of honoring the sacred threads that bind us to the past. This is not merely an ending; it is a powerful prologue to the unwritten chapters that lie ahead – a legacy of light that beckons others to embrace their own call to transformation. Listen, the Ancestors are whispering...

# Priestess Regina "Abegunde" Harris

Priestess Regina "Abegunde" Harris is a naturally committed wife, mother, grandmother, and good sister friend. She is a devoted practitioner of ancestral honoring and serves as a priestess of the Sacred Feminine Mysteries, and in her role as a spiritual midwife guides others along their spiritual journeys.

Over the years her wise womanhood priesthood journey has evolved her into a life coach, spiritual teacher, and soul curator also known as *The Navigator.*

In addition to her spiritual pursuits, she is the director of Grupo Balança of Capoeira in Lexington, Kentucky, a renowned cultural group. She is a passionate advocate for voters' rights who believes in the power of democracy and works to ensure that every voice is heard.

Overall, Priestess Abegunde is a remarkable individual who combines her diverse talents and roles into making a positive impact on the world around her. Her dedication, wisdom, and passion are truly inspiring, and she continues to be a beacon of light for those who have the honor of knowing her.

# The Spiritual Anatomy of a Slave at One with the Light

## Iya Osunnike and Baba Koleoso

### I Remember

Our Priest King Baba Koleoso, (now in the Ancestral Realm) gifted me with 20 years of literally and spiritually taking me around the world and back in ways I never could have imagined.

In this chapter, I'm sharing just a sacred morsel of the ancient Ancestral wisdom that was reawakened deep within our cellular essence and bone marrow while on our first pilgrimage together to West Africa.

Yes, I had a plan in mind for Baba's birthday in Africa. However, be careful what you ask for because the Ancestors had a whole other plan in place. We had no idea what this journey was really going to be about, and the impact that it would have for each and both of us on so many different levels. The revelations that we experienced were actually just a drop in the sea container revealing our destiny and its connection to our past lifetime remembrances and future spiritual leadership callings. Wow, like the saying goes: *you can't make this up*.

This Sankofa/looking back journey opened the portal to guide us in rising up into our sacred spiritual light co-leadership of the Institute of Whole Life Healing even in the darkest times, no matter what. The high vibrational metaphors that were revealed within those pits of darkness continue to this day to reflect the At One to me, as me, and so much more. I Remember...

www.manypaths1truth.org

# Iya Osunnike Remembers

October 1999, I'm back home in Boston after returning from my year long life transforming time living in Jamaica. My spiritual healing practice was now amplified and taking me around the US to provide sacred energy and sound healing sessions along with what was becoming my specialty Multi-dimensional Life Recall (reconnecting to other lifetime) sessions. It also gave me an extraordinary opportunity to connect and collaborate with some other profound spiritual healers and leaders. One of whom constructed a website highlighting my life's mission in support of the ascension of humanity. Shortly after the website was created, I received an email from a High Priest named Baba Koleoso, who lived in Kentucky, and shared how much he resonated with my mission that was being shared on the website and the diversity of the different Priests and our specialties. This was the beginning of a very powerful re-connection to Baba, my Twin Flame, which I didn't know at that time, and would contribute to me weaving together the tapestry of my soul. As a major part of that tapestry, I would also be moving to Kentucky...say what...Kentucky! However, on my first visit to Kentucky when he picked me up from the airport, he said...

# Baba Koleoso Remembers

Osunnike, I want to make sure you have something good to eat, and that you get an interesting taste of Kentucky.

# Iya Osunnike Remembers

I smiled and said jokingly, "That sounds great, as long as it's not Kentucky Fried Chicken."

# Baba Koleoso Remembers

"No worries. Kentucky is a lot more than that chicken. Trust me."

## Iya Osunnike Remembers

I did trust him. He took me to what had been an old plantation that had been restored by a friend of his, as a cultural center and restaurant called the Java House. After eating dinner, Koleoso asked her if she would show me more of this old new space. As I walked through this structure, I could feel the pain – ancestral pain. As Niela escorted me into the backyard, I had to stop in front of this very large tree and kneel. She acknowledged that I was tapping into all the souls who were still energetically trapped, when their bodies were hung from those branches. After what seemed forever, Koleoso lifted me from the ground and we went back inside.

## Baba Koleoso Remembers

He said, "With all the work that we've done here many of those ancestors are still struggling to move on."

## Iya Osunnike Remembers

That's what I felt when she took me up into the attic to show me the different artifacts that had been found on the property. I began to feel angry, as I looked at this long box that looked like a wooden coffin. With my hand shaking and tears in my eyes, I pointed to it and asked, "What is that?" I felt Koleoso place his hand on my back, as he said,

## Baba Koleoso Remembers

"It's a breeding box. The slave masters would select some of the very strong men and very fertile women on the plantation, lock them inside the box and force them to breed."

# Iya Osunnike Remembers

"How the hell could they do that?" I hissed.

# Baba Koleoso Remembers

"If they resisted, they and their family members were tortured or killed; that's how the hell that was done" he said.

# Iya Osunnike Remembers

I had studied a lot about slavery, but I had never heard of breeding boxes. This was horrifying. Now, I was hypnotized by the strong ancestral pulse that ran through the veins of these historic lands. After that night and later saying yes to the divine invitation to move to Kentucky, that ancestral reintroduction for healing and ascension was the beginning of our Institute of Whole Life Healing work around the world together. However, Koleoso was already very much aware of the history associated with Kentucky and had developed Ancestral honoring ceremonies within the community. I had to let him know that transitioning here was somewhat intimidating for me. I remember him saying...

# Baba Koleoso Remembers

"Osunnike, what are you talking about? We are here to do this work together. I've been telling the women that I have worked with over the years, that they need a Priestess with your past lifetime work and womb healing knowledge and skillset to guide them on the next level of their spiritual journeys. That's not my work with them. I am here to uplift these men and restore our divine origins, and to inspire young men and boys to know they're here for a higher purpose. The women need that from you. Let's do this sacred feminine and divine masculine work together." So, we did. And the Ancient Mothers and ancestors kept taking us deeper and deeper into this work. The next thing I knew, the Sankofa (reaching back) was calling us to Ghana to celebrate Baba's earth birthday in the bosom of Mother Africa.

This was our first trip together to Africa; Ghana is one of the primary countries that lost so many of their ancestors as part of the Trans-Atlantic slave trade over 400 years ago. We both knew that we were called as priest to Ghana, as part of our Sankofa to receive our ancient Ancestral Seeds of Wisdom to share with the world. This was also a part of Our Calling in this lifetime to heal our intergenerational trauma and become a unifying bridge from Africa to America and beyond. But we didn't have a clear picture of that back then.

## Baba Koleoso Remembers

I was being "called" to the Elmina Dungeons in Ghana; instructed to spend my 56th earth day in the slave cells. God, Divinities, and the Ancestors opened that door. On Tuesday, February 22, 2005, Osunnike and I landed in Accra, Ghana. I was 'HOME', and my soul knew it, time to sit and ask my Mother Africa, "Why, oh why Mother did you let us go?" On Wednesday, we arrived at Elmina castle. As we walked through this massive space, Osunnike from her intuitive knowing began to pick up the vibrations of what took place in each room. From the roof to the holding cells, we felt the ancestral pain.

## Iya Osunnike Remembers

On that day no one else other than Koleoso and I were there. As I slowly and methodically walked inside the structures that had imprisoned the female slaves, I felt deep pain within my womb along with the necessary strength it took to endure those unfathomable horrific journeys. I could also see their eyes looking back into their villages and hear their voices silently screaming how could you let me go? Those silent screams reverberated from my head to my toes as I desperately was trying to get the answer to that question. Then I heard another voice loudly echoing from somewhere within this darkness as I began to find my way to

Koleoso.

## Baba Koleoso Remembers

Another voice was calling, another vibration pushing through, another reality making itself known. It was a vibration and frequency of determination, liberation, and spiritual ascendance. All of which was a great surprise for us in this dungeon. As Osunnike in a trance like state walked back to me from the female cells, full of tears she said...

## Iya Osunnike Remembers

"Koleoso, I know where so much of the desecration of the sacred feminine began. It began here! I feel the pain of those mothers and their children, violated, lost, and forgotten."

## Baba Koleoso Remembers

Just then, we realized there was a strong female voice calling to us and then 9 Queen Mothers appeared as if out of nowhere! In a matter-of-fact manner, once they saw us, one of them said as she pointed to Osunnike, "We are Queen Mothers from the central region!! We can hear your cries. She must come back to us, now – We remember her."

## Iya Osunnike Remembers

The Queen Mothers instructed us to join them in a ritual of pouring water/libations to our Ancestors at the 'Door of No Return'. In this deep dark space, I swear I began seeing brilliant stars flickering like light beams in the night sky. I felt like I was having flashbacks, and my trauma was transmuting.

# Baba Koleoso Remembers

That Thursday morning, my birthday was full of psychic energy due to the full moon the night before and my own earth day sensitivity. We dressed in white and proceeded back to the castle. This morning I went directly to the male cells while she returned to the female cells. I poured libations and left some DNA there at the 'door of no return'. In the dark, damp cell, I found a place to kneel. I began to pray, and chant and it seemed as if I was reconnecting with ME, a Ghanaian Ancestor who it felt like had failed his people. So, I prayed and chanted even more and then a feeling of great resolve and determination came over me. I realized my other lifetime Ancestor was at peace. He had found a place within himself where he knew that he was going to make it through! With that knowing, I realized that I had become possessed again by that same Ancestor I connected with in 1998 during my initiation as a Shango priest. Now, I realized that Ancestor embodied the Shango energy which represents courage, conviction, and leadership. Also, associated with lightning and the SUN.

Oh, what a grand earth day gift!! As opposed to experiencing anger or hatred, I began to feel great admiration and wondered how my Ancestors survived this! Who were these people? I heard and felt his response, "Who were we? This is what you must figure out. You sit here in this dungeon with all your spiritual knowledge and experiences. Now ask yourself who were we in the spiritual sense? Once you find out, you must let the world know and never forget." I emerged from the dungeons renewed and charged seeking to understand my Ancestors from a spiritual perspective. I have always taken great pride in knowing that we come from Spiritual Royalty who were forced to come here and take that dreaded journey. The following is an effort to begin fulfilling the charge that was given to us by our Ancestors. "The Spiritual Anatomy of a Slave".

# Iya Osunnike Remembers

What I was beginning to realize was that this journey was

mirroring more of our individual and collective other lifetimes and providing us with a healer heal thyself opportunity. Surely, in the pit of my knowing, I was remembering me, yes me in these cells. Yes, now I remembered me in Ghana on that slave ship coming into Jamaica. I realized we Africans who survived the slave dungeons, middle passage, forced confinement, rape and slavery had a tremendous inherent knowing of our spiritual vibrational frequency. That is how we endured and transcended the physical and mental torture and conditionings. Now, I'm remembering the luminous light that moved through our veins and spirit that gave me/us not only the will to survive...to thrive. During those journeys we were being called to look deep enough inside our own minds, bodies and spirits and remember the effort it takes to harvest the fruits of physical and spiritual seeds planted in the darkness of the earth by our ancestors, generations ago?

Intergenerationally we must never forget the cellular genetic memory of being a slave. Now, I'm remembering the blazing resilience that moved through my veins as an enslaved Ghanian Queen Mother who freed herself and others as a Jamaican Maroon woman lifetimes ago. So, I say to you, what level of spiritual transcendence do you think those Ancestors attained? We talk about spiritual transcendence and enlightenment as part of the New Age movement. Well, this is Ancient New Age Knowing that the Ancient Indigenous Ancestors knew and then some. I remember these were the words of the enlightened Ancestors speaking to Koleoso and through him, which cannot be forgotten.

## Baba Koleoso Remembers

As I sat there in the dungeon on my earth day listening to the whispers of my Ancestors, one message was loud and clear, "What of our immune systems? Seek to understand the (Spiritual significance) of our immune systems. I contend that my Ancestors had a clear understanding of their spiritual At-One-Ment with the Primal Source also known as God. It had to have been clear that they were one with this Universal Source. They must have had transcendental experiences with that At-One-Ment and knowing that being At One with the Universal Source is what humanity is the embodiment of.

Now, let us look at this spiritual anatomy a little further. Where does the child get its immune system? The child gets its immune system from the antibodies of the mother; it is these antibodies which help to build the immune system. That being the case, not only were the immune systems of our African Ancestors derived from their physical mothers but from Mother Africa herself. The spiritual milk of Mother Africa was rich in antibodies which warded off disbelief in this Universal Source and our At-One-Ment with God. She knew that she was/is the Mother of us all, that it was she born of the Cosmic Great Mother, Mother Africa who took the cosmic seed of God and gave birth to us all. Just as our African Ancestors suckled from the breast of their mothers or any village mother who was there to nurse them, our Ancestors suckled from the various spiritual traditions within the womb of Mother Africa, all which leads to this experience with the universal At-One-Ment, Source/God.

## Iya Osunnike Remembers

Does not this sound like the knowing of many of the Sages, Rishis, and Swamis? They were clear concerning their ancestral legacy and the stock from which they evolved. It is constantly related to us that individuals who have experienced the universal At-One-Ment are your highly self-realized spiritual beings. As opposed to feelings of anger, those who survived looked to the God of Self for the answers.

## Baba Koleoso Remembers

This spiritual resilience and At-One-Ment is also reflected within the inborn anatomy of the Lotus flower which represents the expansion of consciousness, and transcendence from the lower self to the higher self. The growth of the Lotus' pure resilience from within the mud is a symbol of mental purity and Enlightenment. Consciously embodying "the Light" that you are "at one" with enables one to grow past their own conditioned limitations.

We must continue this Black Lotus Rising journey into the Light of truth and purify the body of murky water within ourselves. We are called to purifying the filth of racism, sexism, religious dogma and give rise to a clear vision and higher frequency of oneness among humanity and transparent understanding of, 'Many Paths, One Truth.' Dear One, as you follow your path and frequency you will be able to tap into your spiritual anatomy and be a vehicle of purification for the society (pond) that you find yourself in.

The Lotus grows in MUD and yet purifies the mud in the end. We say to you, like the Lotus, always move toward the light, that which is divinely correct. The more you follow YOUR path, your frequency and at-one-ment with the light, then like the Lotus you will purify the pond that you are in!

## Iya Osunnike Remembers

Today, I still remember the powerful transformation that took place for me as I was being called to reconnect to my Ancestral Spiritual Anatomy within the female slave dungeons. It has strengthened my mission over these last twenty-five years through the Sacred Feminine Mysteries initiations and sacred sexual healing, and rebirthing ceremonies I have designed as a sacred spiritual light leader. I have returned to consciously assist women with their sexual healing, liberation, and to re-experience their divine connection to The Great Mother, all as part of the journey home to At-One-Ment.

You see my dear sisters we must remember as the daughters of The Great Mother our Spiritual Anatomy and Lotus Nature ensures that we are naturally and energetically infused with the nucleus (blueprint) to procreate goddesses and gods. And, by accessing that storehouse of ancient wisdom deeply embedded within the recesses of your mysterious womb, you will remember that you can manifest Heaven on Earth because "From the Womb of Darkness all Light Comes Forth." Yes, the Spiritual Anatomy of the Sacred Feminine Mysteries resides within "your" holy womb.

And like the Lotus who also carries the genetic mud; cellular memories and imprints of our ancestral lineage and their trauma within our Sacred Wombs stretching seven generations back, we can get stuck in that mud and forget our seeds of ancient wisdom and our true destiny.

However, you are called to remember that no matter what trauma you and/or your ancestors endured you have the Spiritual Anatomy, the Sacred Feminine essence to RISE no matter what – refreshed, cleansed, and purified again and again and again.

## Baba Koleoso Remembers

Yes, I remembered that during my first of 2 near death experiences, while on the other side, I was embraced and comforted by ONE bright light! There was only ONE light on the other side, ONE unconditional love, ONE mercy, and only ONE white light! It is to that ONENESS, that UNITY, that UNCONDITIONAL LOVE that I seek to submit. While on the other side I was made aware that the universe and I were ONE. I became conscious of being conscious, that there was only one consciousness of which we all are a part. I was part of everything and everything was a part of me.

My LEGACY for each of YOU is to stand on the shoulders of our ENLIGHTENED ANCESTORS and promote UNITY, to show the UNITY and ONENESS of all of creation and religious ideals. This is something that they, the Ancestors knew and understood, something of which they have charged me with the legacy to carry forward.

## Iya Osunnike Remembers

Our Priest King Baba Koleoso wholeheartedly believed that as we support our ANCESTORS' Ascension, we must look deeply into how we will vigilantly pay homage and veneration to our Enlightened Ancestral Lineages and the Universal Wisdom THEY Embodied, and that WE are called to "Ascend and Resurrect".

Moving forward, we are now being called to utilize our En-Lightened Ancestral "genetic inheritance" more effectively within our DNA, for the greater good for ourselves, families, communities, humanity, Mother Earth, and the UNIVERSE.

As a Rainbow Colored Many Paths ONE Truth Unifying Bridge; our Priest King believed that WE are being called to LIBERATE Ourselves and Humanity from the "past chains" that Bound and Enslaved OUR African Ancestor Wisdom Keepers, Native American and Indigenous Sacred Land Caretakers and ALL Races and Genders who Honored and Valued Living in Alignment with Mother and Father Earth and Sky.

We are called to Cleanse and Purify those horrific traumas buried within our cellular memory/DNA and reclaim our Royal Inheritance, so that we can Evolve our Ancestral Lineage and Ascend above and beyond the shackles of an "enslaved and devalued mindset." You are the light... let it shine let it shine let it shine.

## Our Black Lotus Rising Prayer
## Ascending from the Dark into the Light

---

Beloved Goddess,
Like the Lotus, assist me to rise above my negative circumstances and mindset so that I may bask in the Light of Divine Truth. Yes, my roots are deep in the murky waters of racism, dualism, sexism, oppression, isolation, and ignorance. Yet, I ask that you out of your divine mercy, keep your light shining on me. I am determined like the Lotus to find my way to the surface, on my way to Self-Realization., Rise Black Lotus Rise!

---

*Listen to songwriter and musician Stephen Wise guiding us into Ascension Ascension*
*youtube.com/watch?v=eTNVUtVqI_4*

# Becoming More Aware
## Preeti Gupta

Becoming more Aware alive alert
To come out of our old habit patterns
We need to be living moment to moment

And we need to be dying moment to moment
Dying means
dropping all impressions of previous moment
Being fresh and alive in every given moment
Away from shadow of judgment, of pain, away from shadow of
desires, away from shadow of hurt, away from shadow of
disappointments, away from shadow of resentment

Dropping it all
moment to moment
being fresh and free
Being light and luminous
Being pure and peaceful
Being simple and saintly

The stage is set for you... All the characters are here for a reason
Plan to come out of this maze
Do not let the world and its offerings consume you or entice you
Detach yourself from your character & form - drop drop drop
and come out clean

# Preeti Gupta

Preeti was born and raised in New Delhi, India, and she and her husband have lived in Lexington Kentucky for the past 30 years. Preeti is a genuine heart soul universal people connector. She is known to naturally and effortlessly weave together like-minded mission driven evolutionary do-gooders from different cultures around the world.

Preeti has a natural love for Spirituality, Meditation, Ayurveda, Art, and Music. She is also a gifted writer and shares her ambient poetic expressions within creative and artistic venues to promote health, wellness, diversity, and spirituality.

In addition, Preeti is a successful real estate agent who enjoys helping her friends and clients to find homes that are in alignment with their whole beingness.

# A Note from the Publisher

## Steph Ritz with RitzBooks.com

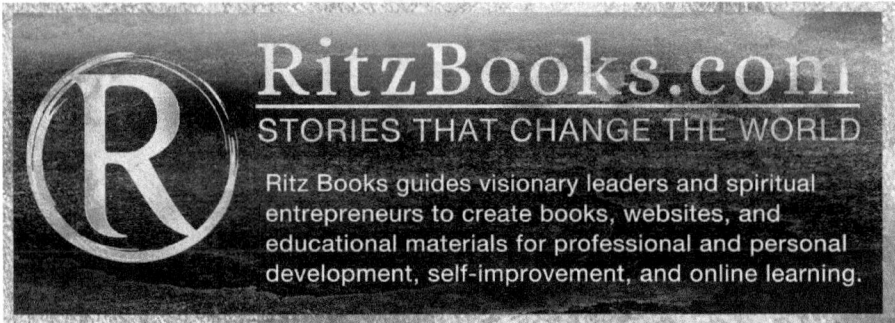

## Steph's Sacred Writing Experiences
## to Inspire Wisdom from Within

Ritz Books brings together authors and artists from around the world to offer you their healing magic. I hope you enjoyed these life-altering messages that celebrate individual differences, who we are at the core, and offers glimpses into our shared humanity.

It is my wish that these books reveal the potential that lies within your heart, uncover possibilities within yourself, and guide you to embrace ultimately creating individual and global transformation. More than that, I wish to offer you a glimpse into the healing magic you have to offer the world.

What you are inspired to write is meant to be shared - not sit inside of you. Please, don't take what lives inside of you to your grave, don't take tomorrow for granted...

Before departing this life, please share your insights, beliefs, and experiences with the world. Take a moment to listen to the voice of your heart and set your wishes sailing in the sky. It's time to leave your legacy.

# Meet Steph Ritz

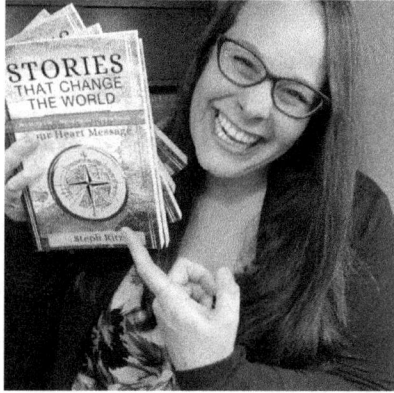

Steph Ritz is the publisher, graphic designer, coach and editor of this book. With dozens of international bestselling books, she is a world-renowned writer, web designer, and photographer. Steph combines cutting-edge writing techniques, deep connection, and taking effective action to create stories that change the world.

Hybrid Publishing with Ritz Books under the imprint "Ritz Books" yet managed from your Amazon account, so you get 100% of the royalties. Collaboration books donate their royalties to non-profits and scholarship funds. Both hybrid publishing and collaborative books include ghostwriting, editing, cover design, and layout.

---

An incredible experience! From start to finish, she created a safe and supportive environment where all participants felt comfortable sharing their stories. I absolutely love my chapter! Even better, the book is phenomenal! I'm amazed at how the stories really do fit together. I highly recommend this collaborative book process to anyone who is looking to get their unique message out to the world and make some incredible connections with like-minded writers. It was a truly transformative experience that I will never forget.

~ Cynthia "Oya Gbemi" Barnes, Esq.

# Ritz Books Authors

Adhana McCarthy, Illinois

Agnes Barna, Sydney, Australia

Angela Heart, California

Annie B. Kay, Massachusetts

Banton Dyer, Texas

Cristina Laskar, California

Cynthia "Oya Gbemi" Barnes, Florida

Dara Bayer, Massachusetts

Debbie Howard, Texas & Japan

Etoke "Fuatabong Lekeanju" Atabong, Maryland & Cameroon, Africa

Glenys Brown, Perth, Australia

Grace Lawrence, Oregon

Hasti Fashandi, California

Ilene Cohen, California

Jay Rooke, California

Jenny McFadden, Sydney, Australia

Jermaine "Spirit Buffalo" Reeves, Kentucky

Julia Lewis, Virginia

Kimberly "Omiseun" Early, Washington

LaVerne "Nzinga" Gyant, Illinois

Lee Blackwell, Lake Macquarie, Australia

Lisa "AyoDeji" Allen, Pennsylvania

Lorna Patten, Cammeray, Australia

Louise Elliott, Canberra Australia

Makhosi Yeye Gogo Nana Omari, Maryland

Mariyamah "OloMidara" Hill-Sanna, Ohio & Ghana, Africa

Marshall "Omitosin" Henderson Jr., Tennessee

Mesfen Manna, Kentucky

Michelle Bee, California

Nashid "Koleoso" Fakhrid-Deen (1949-2020)

Nicole DeAvilla, California

Pat Southern-Pearce, Manchester, United Kingdom

Phyllis Douglass (Vox Angelus), California

Preeti Gupta, Kentucky & New Delhi, India

Radcliffe Johnson, California

Ralph Stevenson, Pennsylvania

Regina "Abegunde" Harris, Kentucky

Robin "Osunnike" Scott-Manna, Kentucky

Robin Daw, California

Roza Bann, Sydney, Australia

Sebastian Laskar, California

Sorcha Fraser-Swatton, Mudgee, Australia

Steph Ritz, California

Tomas Reyes, California & Columbia, South America

Vivian Geffen, Arizona

When tested, we are all stronger than we imagined, smarter than we give ourselves credit for, and have the resiliency of a dandelion... for when the light calls, we will rise again.

~ Steph Ritz